CONTENTS

THE BEGINNINGS OF A HOBBY

THE BRICKS

The blocks were conceived one evening in my cellar. They began as a half-hearted attempt to make a log like those in a set of American Logs that I had during my grammar school years. I wasn't much at either woodworking or perseverance, so my log attempt met with disappointment. The logs from that experiment were neither attractive nor quite what I wanted, so I dropped the project. What I really wanted was a replacement for another childhood building toy — my set of American Plastic Bricks. Unfortunately, I knew I could never make a brick.

I went ten years without a modeling hobby and, during that time, a major part of me was empty. I had never seen anything built with logs other than the pictures on a box, and I couldn't imagine them as a hobby. However, I couldn't think of anything else to make that appealed to me. That first attempt, while a disappointment, was not really a failure. The logs did interlock, they did remain one atop another, and a small structure did result. I dwelled on this for the next year and a half as I wondered if I could, without a clue as to where a pile of logs might lead, proceed with just a little more care and at least be able to make them attractive.

I ultimately began a second, more meticulous, attempt, and was rewarded with an attractive log. This unusual success encouraged me and, as I proceeded with the logs, I chanced on a new shape that wasn't really a log. With that discovery, I renamed the logs and, in that moment, the blocks were born. My journey was just beginning.

I didn't stumble onto the blocks as a hobby entirely by chance. They arose from a conflict I had struggled with since I was a teenager, that between a child and an adult. I think the blocks hobby is a compromise somewhere between the toys I had as a child and the models I had made as an adult.

Our family traveled a lot by train, so I was captivated by trains from early on. We also visited the city of Boston frequently, and I was enamored by it as well. The toys that influenced the blocks came from these childhood adventures.

The earliest toy was an American Flyer train that my father gave me when I was five years old. He was a craftsman and eventually discovered the more craftsman-like HO scale models. His interest in the American Flyer train quickly dwindled, but I continued to relate more to the older toys than to the newer models. Since his interest in trains was primarily for me, the train endeavor eventually collapsed.

The next toy was a set of American Plastic Bricks. When I was nine, I had saved enough of my allowance to buy the first set, and over the next few years I added more sets to the collection. The bricks were fully my own idea and were an attempt to miniaturize my adventures in Boston. The bricks were actually the goal of the blocks.

I had one other construction toy that was a precursor to the blocks — a set of American Logs — that were similar to Lincoln Logs, but had a square profile rather than round. I had only one set and couldn't build much, so I used the logs primarily for indoor scenes. Though the logs meant little to me as a child, they were the only toy of the three that I thought I could replicate. The logs, therefore, gave the blocks their form.

Of all the toys I ever had, only the bricks and their entourage of miniature figures and vehicles remain. The brick assemblages that follow were put together for this book from memory and a few photographs. In my early years, the bricks could represent almost anything. In addition to assembling houses, I used the bricks as people and to make entire cities. With the blocks, though, all the fanciful scenes are gone. My only attempt has been to replicate this ultimate city scene, and many of the block shapes were designed as replacements for specific bricks or constructions.

FIGURE 01-01: The square half-bricks are soldiers and the rectangular full bricks their mounts. The white coping blocks are chevrons; one for junior officers and two for senior. The white bricks are full and double length lintels and were used as wagons. The angular gable bricks were loose fitting on the high end and were used as the harness between horses. Some of the lowly privates got to ride in the wagon, but had to function as the tongue and traces as well.

FIGURE 01-02: Here, the white double lintels topped with a single lintel are modern locomotives. The off-white bricks at the lower and upper left are older steam locomotives. The full red bricks were freight cars, and the double and triple lintels without a topping were passenger cars. As with the cavalry, the gable bricks were connectors, couplers in this case.

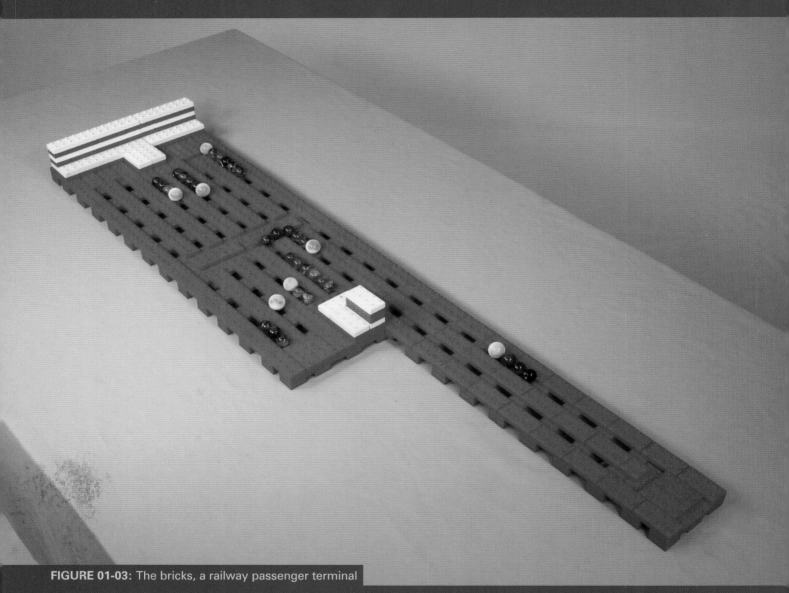

FIGURE 01-03: The bricks, a railway passenger terminal

FIGURE 01-03: This railway passenger terminal is based on my experiences at Boston's South Station. I somehow discovered that two rows of bricks separated by a quarter unit would allow a marble to roll smoothly between them. With a framework underneath, the bricks became railroad tracks. The photo shows a double track line entering at the lower right, a double track throat crosswise in the middle, six platform tracks in the rear, and a yard for baggage and storage at the front. A single course of red bricks topped by a course of white lintels represents a building story in these scenes. The large marbles represent locomotives, the orange cat's eyes baggage cars, and the blue cat's eyes coaches. One train is arriving and another is rounding the bend to depart from the throat. A number of orange baggage cars are being loaded at the baggage terminal, and a locomotive and three blue coaches are idle in the yard.

FIGURE 01-04: Here is a similar theme as FIGURE 01-03, but with trolley cars. In addition to accommodating marbles, I found that the space between the brick pegs would perfectly guide a Renwal vehicle. I kept all my Renwal vehicles since they were part of the brick entourage. The station very loosely represents Lechmere Station in Cambridge. Lechmere was actually a loop with only one or two sidings, but it was located at the bottom of an incline from a viaduct. The actual trains frequently ran in pairs, and I used safety pins to couple the cars as shown in the foreground. A two-car train of delivery vans, i.e., trolleys, is crossing the throat to the platform on the left. In this larger scale, three red courses capped by a course of lintels represent a story.

FIGURE 01-05: The bricks, a city

FIGURE 01-05: An entire city with a single brick representing a story. The red half bricks were houses and were rarely more than three stories high. Other combinations of red bricks represented older buildings, and the white lintels were more modern. Sufficient structure density was required in order to delineate the streets. The white coping blocks were buses, and I tried to include enough to suggest the routes. The green roofs were parks, and the red gable bricks were subway entrances. One subway entrance is shown in the park in the center, and another pair is in the park at the right. The subway routes can only be determined by locating the entrances, much as in some city maps I've seen.

FIGURE 01-06: The bricks, a wharf scene

FIGURE 01-06: This wharf scene is based on Atlantic Avenue in Boston. For the first time, we see gable bricks actually being used as gables. As a result, the coping blocks became the connecting hawsers. In these scenes, red bricks with gables are the older warehouses, and one or two red courses capped by a course of white lintels represent the newer buildings. Tugboats always looked the same — four full red bricks, one of which was crosswise, topped by a half brick. Three tugs are shown at the bottom: One towing a barge, one at the dock, and one heading toward an oceangoing vessel at the right. Smaller boats and another liner are tied up at the docks. Over the course of an evening, these waterfront scenes could become quite extensive.

FIGURE 01-07: The bricks, a downtown scene

FIGURE 01-07: This is an example of the ultimate scenes from my high school years. In these scenes, the bricks are used as designed except that the cardboard roof pieces represent streets and lawns as well as roofs. The vehicles in the water at the left — my desk was normally water — are actually in a staging area. The wooden boat at the front is a replica of a boat I made while in grammar school. I have a photo of a town I set up in our attic that includes the original. The upper walkways, terraces, underpass, and clutter are taken from my trips to Boston's market district.

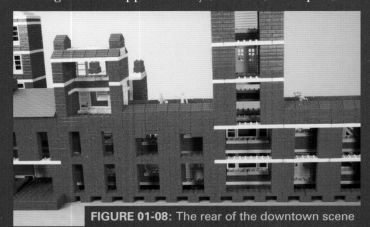

FIGURE 01-08: The rear of the downtown scene

FIGURE 01-08: The rear view of FIGURE 01-07. The rear of my oak desk abutted a bureau, so the rear of any display was hidden. Therefore, except as needed for stability, I omitted the rear walls.

FIGURE 01-09: The cartoon character Wimpy normally piloted the boat. I never did learn the name of the little green man. His hat was originally much longer, giving him the tendency to overturn, so I lopped it off. Jiggs, another cartoon character, is on one of the terrace walkways.

FIGURE 01-09: The alley

FIGURE 01-10: The wharf framework

FIGURE 01-11: The underpass

FIGURE 01-10: This is the standard framework I used for piers and streets. This combination of bricks was the minimum height needed to represent a pier: Two courses in one orientation and a single course in the other. This view also shows a garage door in the open position.

FIGURE 01-11: The underpass and a garage door in the closed position. The roof on the overpass is flanked by walls on both sides. This view also points out the difficulty with bricks as walkways. The coping blocks were intended to adorn roofs, and were in scant supply for walks. I had only enough for the terrace walks in this scene.

FIGURE 01-12: Gable roofs flanked by one and two walls

FIGURE 01-12: The open back and a roof flanked by a wall on only one end. It also shows some inverted bricks being used as a chimney.

FIGURE 01-13: Coping blocks used as walkways

FIGURE 01-13: This shows the use of coping blocks as walkways, both on the terrace and on the walkways connecting the upper stories of buildings.

THE TRAIN

While the bricks period of my youth was the origin of the blocks, the early adult train period was for the most part an evolutionary dead-end. However, it's from this period that the block rules evolved, so the train years weren't entirely a waste.

After high school, I spent another year and a half at home before leaving for good. My brick structures were now more formal, sometimes experimental, and never represented anything but bricks. I considered enhancing the bricks with wooden bridges, but I dropped the idea for lack of skill and patience. I also wasn't sure I wanted more bricks. Even with additions, the hobby seemed like a dead-end. The Halsam Products Company, manufacturer of the bricks and logs, was out of business. The A. C. Gilbert Company was also gone, so the American Flyer train also appeared dead.

As my interest in the bricks declined, my interest in a model railroad increased. I bought a ready-to-run Varney HO scale train set and some Atlas snap track. However, it wasn't until I had left home that I began what is called serious model railroading. My first project was a 2 x 8-foot table over the bed in my apartment. I would go home on the weekends and use my father's radial arm saw to build the table. The layout was a simple yard laid with flex-track with a plaster cliff in the rear. I envisioned an eventual around-the-room layout, but I had no specific plan.

Shortly after leaving home, I married Carol, who I had been dating for about a year. It wasn't long after our marriage that I assembled the last structure with the bricks — a skyscraper — on the kitchen table in our apartment. At about the same time, I made two conscious decisions: One, it was time to become an adult; and two, adults don't play with bricks. I was twenty-five years old when I reluctantly set the bricks aside. I encouraged Carol to help me with the HO layout, and together we landscaped the grassy area at the top of the cliff, me laying sawdust grass and she planting clove cabbages to make a little garden.

After we purchased a home, I bought a radial arm saw of my own, along with a portable drill, a saber saw, a circular saw, and an orbital sander. For the next twenty-five years, these were the only power woodworking tools I had. Once our family was established, I began a permanent HO scale model railroad in the basement. While this was a positive step for me, it terminated Carol's interest in the hobby. No matter where I'd place the original apartment yard in my plan, it didn't fit, so I decided to scrap it. The decision seemed logical to me, but Carol doesn't like to toss an item once created. As the cabbage patch died, so did Carol's interest in the railroad. She never made anything for the train after that.

Ironically, by way of a school event, Carol introduced me to another model railroader, and I joined an informal group to which he belonged. Through them, I learned about the social and political aspects of model railroading and had the opportunity to visit many layouts. Although I must have known such things existed, I was particularly impressed with layouts in the larger O scale. I was also surprised to find that many adult males built and operated O gauge Lionel railroads. I was even more surprised to discover that great quantities of S gauge American Flyer equipment was still available at train shows. The disturbing aspect of these discoveries was that I still preferred these larger, often toy-like railroads to the more meticulously built HO layouts.

After about ten years, with the HO railroad completely encircling the cellar, my doubts consumed me. I liked the unfinished sections of the railroad more than those with scenery. I found that once the grass and delicate trees were in place, and particularly a short section of catenary, the railroad became both untouchable and un-cleanable. In scale model railroading, realistic scenery is the ultimate visual goal, but the closer I got to the goal, the more distant the railroad became. I've never thought of myself as possessing envy, but I must say that I envied those modelers with the larger toy trains.

I finally reached a point where I couldn't continue, and after a wrenching internal debate and over Carol's dismayed objection, I ripped up the railroad. I fully intended to build a new HO layout and even made two unsuccessful attempts, but I couldn't get past the feeling that HO was too small. It simply wasn't suited to my un-verbalized preference for toy-like modeling. In fact, I don't think I've ever seen a toy-like HO layout. Craftsmanship varies, but it doesn't' seem often that someone sets out deliberately to create a stylized HO railroad.

THE BICYCLE

Just as the destruction of the cabbages had turned Carol away from the railroad, the destruction of the HO layout was final for me. If I were ever to have another railroad, the destruction issue would have to be addressed.

The demolition of the railroad marked the beginning of what might be called the cycling period. During this time, I had no modeling hobby at all, but cycling gave me lots of time to think. I constantly dreamed of a railroad, and a set of rules for a new layout evolved in my mind. The following four rules — drawn from the good and bad of the American Flyer train, the American Plastic Bricks, and the HO scale railroad — were to form the basis of any future modeling endeavor. The blocks, though not yet conceived, probably had their beginning from these rules.

1. **EVERYTHING MUST BE FUN.** Much of the scale modeling I did for the HO railroad was to please some unspecified other person. Nearly every activity involves components we don't enjoy, but I was determined to keep these to a minimum.

2. **EVERYTHING MUST BE ELEMENTAL.** The waste that resulted from the destruction of the layout led me to decide that whatever I made must be reusable. There was to be no track rendered useless a second time because it had been curved and ballasted. There was to be no structure that had no place on the next layout. There was to be no module like the apartment rail yard that would not fit on a new railroad. This rule even applied to the tables that support the hobby. They must be flexible — up, down, sideways, front, and back. It seemed that the best way to make a component reusable was to make it elemental. I occasionally bend the elemental rule, but I try to bend it consciously.

3. **EVERYTHING MUST BE TOUCHABLE.** I guess touch is as important as sight. It was always fun to have a couple of bricks in one hand to slip into a hole while lifting a wall to make a space with the other.

4. **EVERYTHING MUST BE CLEANABLE.** This rule derives from the nights when the railroad group met in my basement. Before each meeting, I vacuumed the cellar. I also vacuumed the entire layout while carefully avoiding an ever-increasing number of completed sections. It's often possible to determine the construction sequence of a layout just by observing the dust.

Though the cycling period yielded a set of rules, I still didn't have anything I could touch. The HO detritus remained intact and I was still searching for a replacement. I missed both the bricks and the train, and for the first time thought of them together. Despite the thousands of boxed dollars in the cellar, I determined that the scale of a railroad had to be larger and that something like the bricks had to be involved. Since I couldn't face the HO remains, I decided to tackle the bricks.

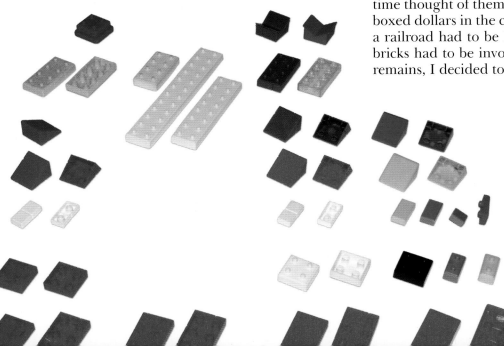

SECTION ONE
THE BASIC BLOCKS

CHAPTER ONE
THE BEGINNING

Once I decided to start with the bricks rather than the train, I was free to focus on the specific form they would take. I knew I could never make a brick, so I had to come up with a simpler interlocking scheme.

The old egg carton method whereby slots are cut halfway through two pieces of cardboard and the pieces slipped together seemed possible. I once had a set of slotted wood pieces from a grab bag that could make a couple of tiny houses in this manner. I didn't have much luck envisioning multiple stories, however, so I didn't pursue the idea. I did most of my daydreaming while cycling, but instruments and a drafting table were probably required to flesh out the egg carton design.

I also wondered about bricks with only two holes and loose rather than glued pegs. This seemed more promising than the egg carton method, but I feared a drill press would be required. Also, the miniscule pegs might violate the cleanable rule.

The interlocking method I finally decided to try was one that had been used in the American Log set. Even while pedaling the bicycle, I could envision myself making logs for a house. The only tool that appeared necessary was the radial arm saw. I wasn't confident I could go anywhere with a set of logs, but I had to start with something that I could at least manufacture.

I had piles of scrap 1 x 2 pine boards left over from the HO train tables, so I had no shortage of material. On the first evening, with some of the straightest boards from the pile in hand, I chose the dimensions. The 1 x 2 boards are about 3/4" thick, so I easily chose that for the height. With the radial arm saw, I could rip a 3/4" width, so I chose that for the width. If the width was 3/4", it was natural then that the notches would be about the same, with half the board's height devoted to the notch depths of 3/16".

The American Log set was long gone and its contents a hazy memory by the time I made a log, so without the benefit of either picture or memory, I chose the lengths. With notches of 3/4", I chose 1-1/2" for the shortest length, then 3" for the next, 4-1/2" for the next, and 6" for the longest. I envisioned 9" and 12" lengths, but didn't get that far.

During the train period, I had become reasonably good at simple carpentry. However, I had little experience with repetitive cuts. In those first evenings, I would measure a length, make the cut, and then mark successive logs from the first for the remainder. The notches involved multiple passes with the 1/8" blade, and each notch varied. I'd seen the word "dado," but had no idea what it meant; also, I had never used nor thought of a stop. Despite this, the logs interlocked, and by the end of one week's time I had enough for a rustic hut. The experiment was sloppy, but the result was a building. Between the sloppiness and the lack of having a vision, however, I decided to give up. The entire week of evenings had yielded barely enough logs for a shed in the woods, so I put them in a little box and went back to cycling. *Sometimes when we envision a new activity, our mind leaps to a grand achievement, but after the first session, we're disillusioned by the effort involved and quit before we've really begun. The initial hubris is followed either by quitting or by an interminably long period of education. It's a point where quitting is easier than continuing, where success departs from failure.*

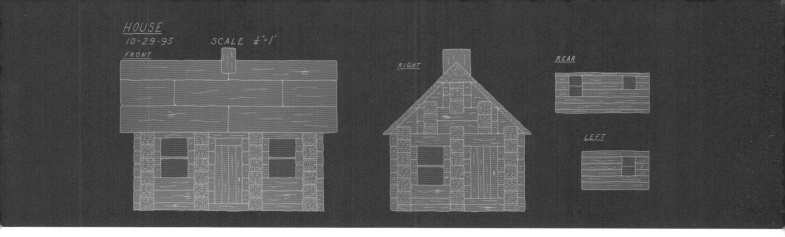

As it turned out, that first week wasn't a total waste. It did give me some concrete problems to think about over the next year and a half. Ripping on the radial arm saw terrified me. At such narrow widths, when the blade encountered a knot, the board would morph into a spear that flew across the cellar. I allowed this to happen only once. Knots were banished. To avoid ripping on the radial arm saw, I decided to try the circular saw with a guide. It would be less accurate but safer, and I could use it outside. With so many cuts, dust was a problem. I somehow discovered the wobble dado, which would permit a single pass for the notches. I also thought of using a stop to ensure exact lengths. Up to this point in my woodworking experience, ripping had been minimal, dust had been minimal, knots an inconvenience, and duplicate lengths normally limited to four, such as a set of legs. By far, however, my biggest problem was patience, and this required nothing but a resolution to increase it.

The second session — a year and a half after the first — began with a surprise. I took a board from the scrap pile, checked it to be sure it was 3/4" thick, and began cutting. After making a few logs, I retrieved the earlier batch. I built a little shack, but unlike the first building, it didn't sit well. It was vertically wavy. I checked the first logs against the new batch and found that the first were 25/32" thick. I had chosen those boards specifically because they had been the straightest and smoothest I had. Precise thickness had never been an issue with the train. I charged around the basement measuring boards and found that of all those in the cellar, the 25/32" group was the anomaly. I also found

that even those that were 3/4" thick weren't precisely so. They varied. I had no way to sand the 25/32" logs, so as far as quantity was concerned, the first session had been a waste. The two sessions combined, however, did provide me with my first dimension — the height must be exactly 3/4".

The second session ended the cycling period. The hobby still had no direction, but now at least it had a solid form. I concluded the cycling period with a few attractive logs and a set of rules by which to manufacture them.

CHAPTER TWO
THE TOOLS & MATERIALS

Other than what I learned from my father and the HO railroad, my woodworking skills are limited to what I have learned from the blocks. As a result, the tools, materials, and methods I use were chosen primarily from my own trials and experiences.

However, you shouldn't feel that you need to rush out and buy all of these at once. I accumulated the tools and jigs over a number of years and haven't yet bought a tool until I came up with a block design that seemed to require it.

WOOD: I use **clear pine** with as few knots and gummy areas as possible. Pine is readily available, easy to work, rarely causes splinters, and the saw blades remain sharp for quite a long time. Also, pine doesn't seem to cause allergies. The exact 3/4" thickness is essential, so I measure each board in a number of places to be sure it's reasonably uniform when I buy it. I used to get thicker and thinner boards from a specialty shop, but recently I began making the odd thicknesses myself. I use **basswood** for carving and modeling since it can be cut with a knife as well as sawed.

RADIAL ARM SAW: When I began with the blocks, the only stationary power tool I had was the radial arm saw, and it became my primary block-making tool. It's excellent for cutting blocks to length, and with a **dado blade set** it's excellent for cutting notches and ripping grooves. I originally bought a wobble dado for the notches, but it was difficult to adjust. A full dado set is a better investment. The radial arm saw can also be used for ripping stock to the desired width, but narrow widths require special securing methods. I prefer a table saw for this operation, but originally used a portable circular saw with a guide.

DUST COLLECTOR WITH EXTRA HOSES: Since blocks are made in vast quantities, this is essential. **Dust masks** and **ear protectors** are also essential. My dust collector makes an incredible racket, so I relegated it to an adjacent room; hence, the extra hoses.

BELT SANDER: I use this for finishing and reducing blocks to the final dimension. I found it easiest to cut blocks to the nominal dimension and then sand them to the final dimension. The belt sander trivializes the sanding operation, making sanding actually fun. The belt sander can also be used for minor shaping operations.

TABLE SAW: While I prefer the radial arm saw for cross cuts, a table saw is easier to use for ripping. The table saw came with instructions for making an **auxiliary fence**, a **push block**, and a **push stick** for narrow rips. I religiously manufactured these and use them all regularly. I have a step stool with a back that's about the height of the table saw that I use as a **table extension** to receive the ripped boards. As a team, the radial arm saw and the table saw make cutting and ripping fun.

ROUTER AND TABLE: I use the router to cut slots in a block for windows and doors. The table came with an elaborate guide mechanism, but I found it awkward for small pieces and don't use it. I did make a **face shield** that consists of a plastic sheet screwed to a board, and I clamp the shield to the table between my face and the router bit.

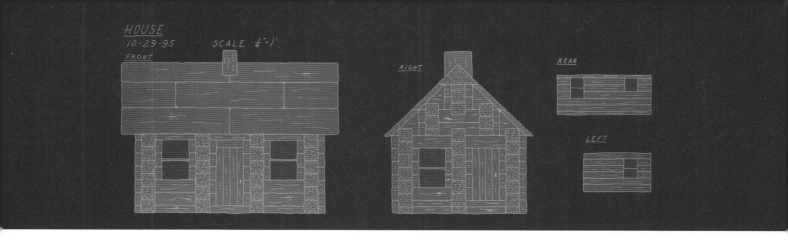

FIGURE 02-01: Saw blades and guides

FIGURE 02-01 shows the blades and guides I use with the radial arm and table saws. Left to right: A combination blade for cross cuts and rips, part of a dado blade set for notches and grooves, and a plastic blade for windows. At the top rear are a rip fence and a push stick for the table saw. Given the narrow widths of blocks, the auxiliary rip fence is almost always required. To their right is a push stick for the radial arm saw with a plywood cap to hold down 3/4" boards when making grooves. Plastic sheets don't take marking very well, so I use the stick at the far right to measure the stop distances. The folding ruler above it would probably do just as well, but I never thought of it.

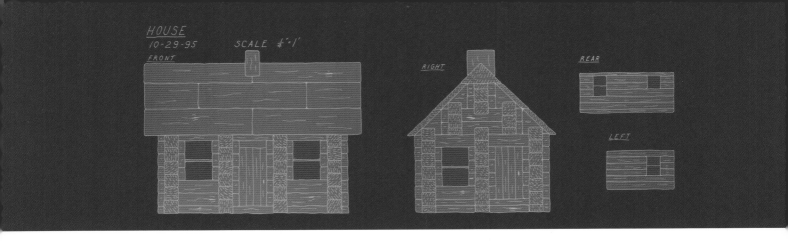

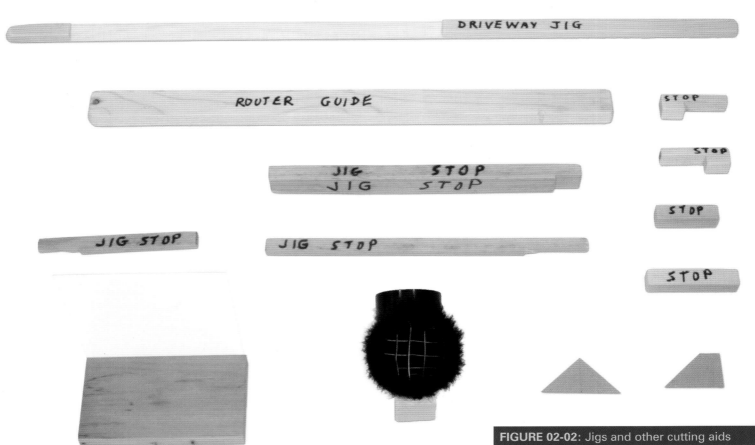

FIGURE 02-02: Jigs and other cutting aids

At the top of FIGURE 02-02 is a 3/8" strip that I placed against the radial arm saw backstop to dado the slope of a driveway. In front of it is the backstop for the router. It has a rabbet on one edge to keep dust from altering the measurements. To the right are the stops I use for the router. Below the router backstop are thick and thin stops for the radial arm saw with notches to, again, keep dust from altering the measurements. In the left foreground is the face guard for the router. In the middle foreground is one of two dust collector brushes. I drilled holes and inserted wires in this one to make a 1/2" square mesh so that I don't lose blocks when using the belt sander. A number of lost blocks prompted this innovation. When I first got the belt sander, I recorded each lost block, and when the dust collector bag was full, I retrieved them. To my dismay, each one had been smashed to ruin by the fan. At the lower right are two templates I use when making the roof profiles. I save almost everything I make. Reusing is easier than remaking.

SAFETY PRECAUTIONS

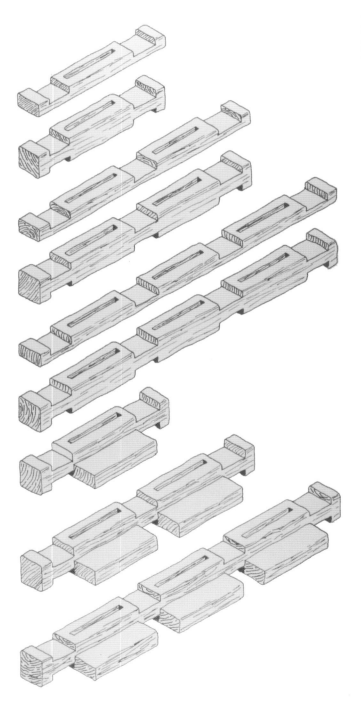

In addition to the safety rules that come with the tools, I have found a few that apply particularly to block-making. Most of these apply to the radial arm saw and router.

- I purchase eight- or ten-foot long boards and cut them to shorter lengths before ripping. Since the blocks are small, there's no need to work with extreme lengths.

- I occasionally design a block that I cannot manufacture, or envision manufacturing, safely. This always requires a design change.

- I've found that if a cut bucks, it's a sure bet that the next cut will buck as well and that an operation change is required. If a dado cut bucks, it's best to try multiple passes rather than risking a second buck.

- I make the smaller blocks in pairs or multiples so that my fingers are a little away from the blade. I try to hold the piece so that it would slip out of my hand rather than taking my hand with it. Notches can act as hooks. For small blocks, I make the notches before the block is cut off, as cross cuts are less apt to buck than dado cuts.

- With the router, I'm religious about cutting only 1/8" at a pass to avoid straining the bit. I pre-drill the ends of the slots, use stops, try to keep the piece between my hands and the bit, and concentrate more than usual on the cuts. As with other small blocks, I often make these in pairs or multiples so that my hands are well away from the bit.

CHAPTER THREE

THE FUNDAMENTALS

It's usually easier to improve an idea than to conceive it in the first place, and the logs were no exception. With the manufacturing improvements behind me, I was able to concentrate on making logs for a building. Over the next two or three years, I experimented with designs for the building components, platforms, and streets. Each block type has a history, but the types weren't designed in a linear order. I'd flit from one type to another; as a result, their development progressed randomly. Some designs finalized immediately; others are uncertain even today, seventeen years into the hobby. For clarity, each block type is discussed as if its design proceeded from the start to its current form in a smooth transition. The actual chronology wasn't so smooth. The basic principles took me years to comprehend, but are likewise grouped as a single topic.

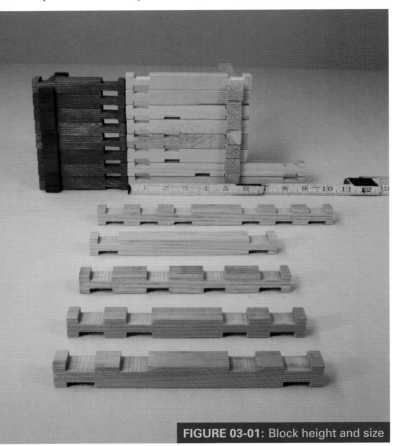

FIGURE 03-01: Block height and size

FIGURE 03-01 shows a stack of early logs placed behind a ruler; the ruler gives an idea of their size.

To their left is a stack of current 3/4" thick Wall Blocks. The early logs are a tad thicker, and the difference in stack height shows how quickly height differences multiply. Fortunately, for most block types, height is the only precise dimension. The logs in the early stack are six and nine inches long. I found these lengths difficult to work with, so I abandoned them.

The logs in the foreground show various notch spacing experiments. I originally tried to locate notches only where needed in a structure, such as those for a custom home. For constantly recycled models, however, I found it easier to have all possible notches in all the blocks. Except for the logs with notches at every location and notches solely at the ends, the other spacing arrangements were abandoned.

When I finally had enough longer logs to make a house, I discovered that no matter how I arranged them, I couldn't position a door opening in the center. This baffled me, so I went outside our Cape Cod home and counted the spaces: Wall, window, wall, door, wall, window, wall. Seven. I had heretofore perversely refused to think of the American Logs, but was now forced to acknowledge them. The longest logs in that set had four notches and three spaces, or seven units. My six- and nine-inch logs were, while of convenient lengths, useless when trying to center a door. The number seven was tough for me to embrace, and it was a long time before I uniformly adopted it. For the basic logs, however, it seemed the only way to proceed.

FIGURE 03-02
THE UNIT AND THE GRID

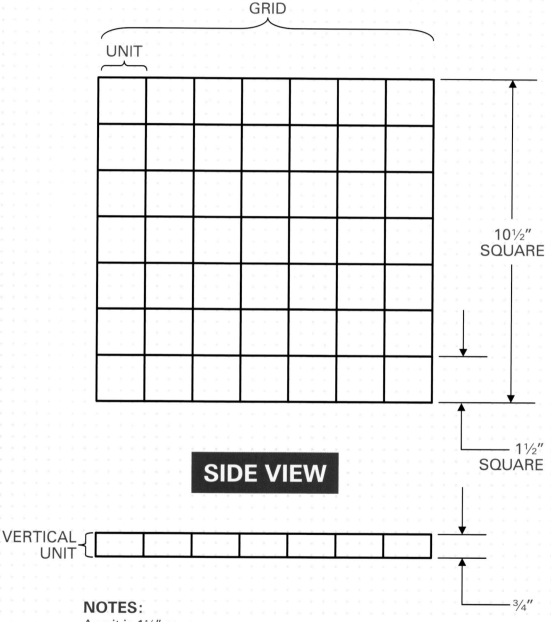

TOP VIEW

GRID

UNIT

10½"
SQUARE

1½"
SQUARE

SIDE VIEW

VERTICAL
UNIT

¾"

NOTES:
A unit is 1½" square.
A grid is 10½" square, (seven units square), and has no height component.
A vertical unit (height unit) is ¾" high.

FIGURE 03-02: This is what I call the **unit** and the **grid**. It was more than a year before I formally named these concepts, but they are the essence of all block dimensions and constructions. The unit, 1-1/2" square by 3/4" high, is the nominal size of the smallest full blocks. To distinguish lengths from heights, I use the term **vertical unit** for height dimensions. It took me a very long time, but I've found that any block that oversteps or fails to reach a unit will have problems with its neighbors. The grid, based on the centered door, is seven units square and has no height component. It's possible to offset adjacent grids, but special constructions are always required. The unit and the grid are essential to understanding the blocks. I changed the name "logs" to "blocks" in conjunction with the grid discovery and have referred to all the shapes as blocks ever since.

FIGURE 03-03

WALL-1 BLOCK DIMENSIONS

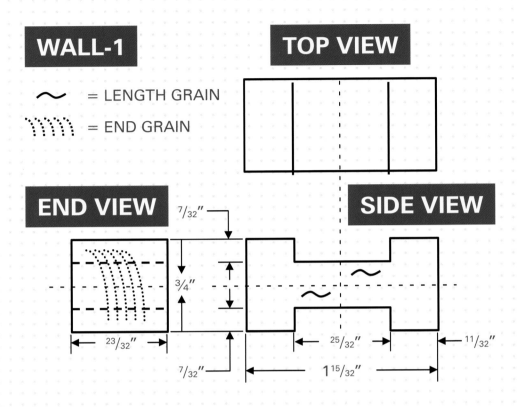

WALL-1

~ = LENGTH GRAIN

))))) = END GRAIN

TOP VIEW

END VIEW

SIDE VIEW

7/32"

3/4"

23/32"

7/32"

25/32"

1 15/32"

11/32"

NOTES:

Measurements on the side view should be oriented from the center of the block so that blocks placed end to end will interlock with those above and below without binding.

The 3/4" height dimension should be as close to exact as possible, as height variations quickly multiply. However, it's not necessary to use calipers.

The 1 15/32" length is approximate, and is intended to fit within a grid so that blocks placed end to end won't bind.

The 25/32" notch dimension is approximate, and is intended to produce a loose fit with the adjoining block.

The 23/32" width dimension is approximate, and is intended to produce a loose fit with the adjoining notches. The 23/32" block width coupled with the 25/32" notch width yields about a 1/16" gap.

The 7/32" notch depth is approximate, and is intended to produce a loose fit with the adjoining block. If the notch is too shallow, adjoining blocks will rest on the notches rather than on the block surfaces.

FIGURE 03-03: The first shapes to be fully developed were the walls, and these are equivalent to logs. This figure shows the basic Wall Block dimensions. The only exact dimension is the height. Note that the lengths are measured from the centerline rather than from the ends. This is critical in order to avoid binding between adjacent blocks.

FIGURE 03·04

THE UNIT AND GRID VS.
WALL BLOCK DIMENSIONS

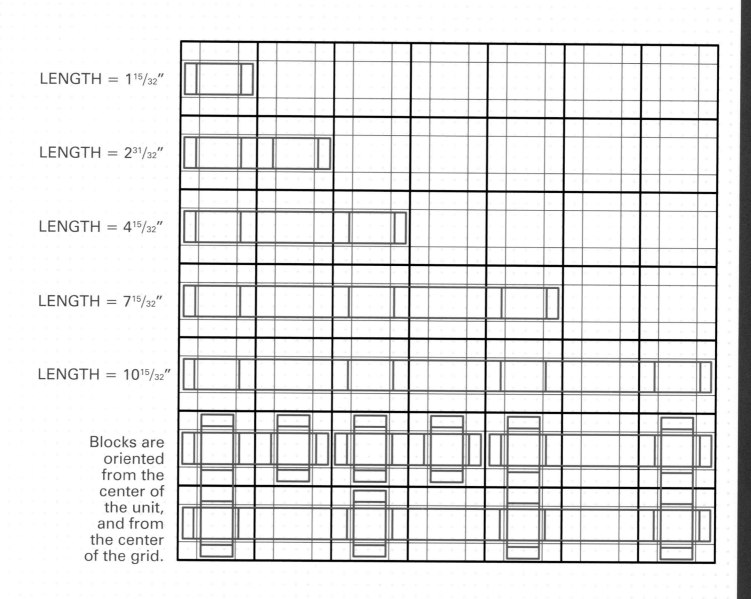

LENGTH = $1^{15}/_{32}''$

LENGTH = $2^{31}/_{32}''$

LENGTH = $4^{15}/_{32}''$

LENGTH = $7^{15}/_{32}''$

LENGTH = $10^{15}/_{32}''$

Blocks are oriented from the center of the unit, and from the center of the grid.

FIGURE 03-04: This shows how Wall Blocks fit inside the unit and the grid. Note that the blocks are both narrower and shorter than the unit or grid within which they fit. The notches in the seven-unit long block at the bottom of the grid align with those of the three shorter blocks above so that the short crosswise blocks will properly interlock.

FIGURE 03-05

NOMINAL VERSUS
ACTUAL DIMENSIONS

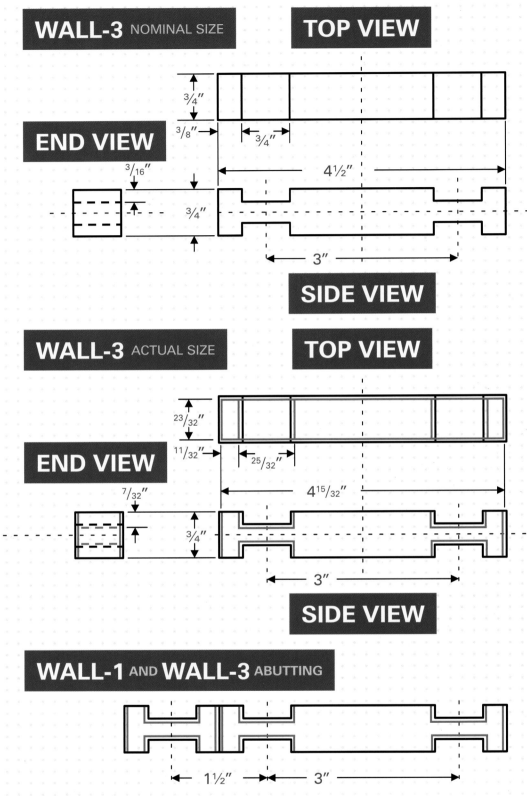

WALL-3 NOMINAL SIZE — **TOP VIEW**

END VIEW

SIDE VIEW

WALL-3 ACTUAL SIZE — **TOP VIEW**

END VIEW

SIDE VIEW

WALL-1 AND **WALL-3** ABUTTING

FIGURE 03-05: This shows how nominal dimensions relate to actual dimensions. Note that the only exact dimensions are the height and the distance between the notch centerlines. It may seem that I've harped too much on these dimensions, but many binds led to their adoption. My earliest blocks were notched with a combination blade and without a stop. I occasionally encounter a block that's too wide coupled with one with notches too narrow. I then have to rearrange the blocks to get a pair that fits. Fortunately, these blocks are of a slightly different design and are stored separately from the current blocks.

NOTES:

The only exact dimensions on the actual block are the ¾" height and the 3" distance between the centerlines of the notches. All other actual dimensions are intended to be as close to the nominal dimension as easily possible without binding. I've found that $1/32$" is about the smallest dimension that's easy to work with. This gives about $1/16$" play when connecting two blocks. This also allows for the slightest amount of bending or bowing in the longer blocks.

BLOCK NAMING

When I'm building a little house, I don't think of blocks by name. "I need a handful of these, two of those, and a few of these" is sufficient. This is fine for building, but less useful in a "Bill of Materials." Consequently, the first bill of materials led to my first attempt at naming. In the early period, I was most concerned with dimensions and notches, so the first names attempted to capture these features. The name had to capture the block type, its length, width, and height, the number of notches, its color, its orientation, and its use. The name B311-5W-BEAM described a block that was three units long, one unit high, and one unit wide. It had five notches, was wood colored, and was a beam. The same block today has the name BEAM-3-W. This describes a basic block, three units long, wood colored, and that is used as a beam. A beam by its name alone defines a basic block, one unit wide and high, of a certain notch pattern, that is used as a beam. The only variations in a Beam Block are the length and color.

If a block fits the description of two or more block types, I usually choose the earlier block type for the name. WALL-1 and BEAM-1 Blocks would be identical, so WALL-1 is the name for a one unit block with a single pair of notches.

The current names include system, version, name, sub-name, variations, and color. A key to the block naming and a complete list of the basic block types appear in the Appendix at the back of this book. For the common types, called "Basic," the names are quite simple.

One thought that consumed me during the late cycling period was the scale for a new model railroad. The blocks, by the mere selection of their dimensions, ended this problem and dictated the scale for the railroad. If a one-unit width was a doorway, then three feet would be about right for a one-unit-long block. Five vertical units equaled 7-1/2 feet, which is about right for a door with a transom. The 1-1/2" length would equal three feet, and **1/2" per foot would be the scale for the blocks**. Very little model railroad equipment is available in 1/2" scale. Fortunately, G scale is just a bit larger and is awash in equipment, so I chose that for the railroad scale.

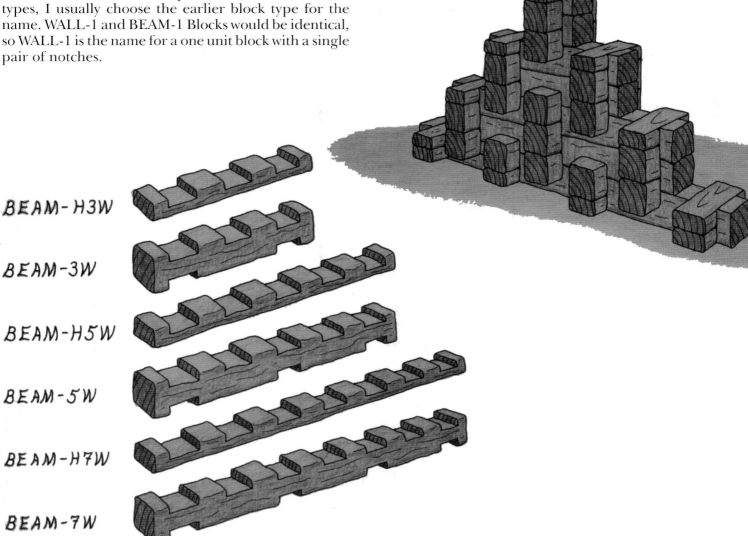

BEAM-H3W

BEAM-3W

BEAM-H5W

BEAM-5W

BEAM-H7W

BEAM-7W

CHAPTER FOUR
WALL BLOCKS

Wall Blocks were the first blocks that I developed and are copied from the design in the American Log set. Though intended as copies, I didn't remember the originals and went through three design stages before arriving at the American Log design. The first was the length problem wherein I couldn't center a door, the second was the varying notch patterns for a single length, and the third was an attempt to incorporate a window casing.

The American Log set didn't have windows or doors. Since I wanted these, I tried to design a log to accommodate them. My first attempt at a window casing was to cut a vertical slot in the ends of each block with a portable saber saw. A sheet of clear plastic or cardboard could then be slipped between the blocks on each side of a window opening. I made and stained a number of logs using this design, but hadn't yet designed a window or door, so I never used those logs as casings. The slots gave the block ends a cluttered look, so I ultimately abandoned the design. I still use the blocks, but keep them separate from those of the current design.

In FIGURE 04-01, Sara looks at the current collection of Wall Blocks.

From front to rear, their lengths are one, two, three, five, and seven units. Each has both a half and full vertical unit height size. I use four colors for Wall Blocks, but only the clay and wood colored blocks come in all sizes. At the left rear is a building comprised entirely of Wall Blocks. For the roof, three WALL-5-W Blocks fit into notches, and two WALL-5-W Blocks fit loosely between notches.

My refusal to check a Lincoln Log set before making the Wall Blocks led me to keep the WALL-2 and WALL-2H Blocks, those third and fourth from the front in the collection. This length doesn't seem to be included in the Lincoln Log sets.

The low wall at the left is comprised of abutting WALL-7-W Blocks, which are tied together by offset WALL-2-W and WALL-2H-W Blocks. **Offset ties** are the basic method for connecting abutting blocks that are longer than two units. The WALL-2 Block is so basic to block constructions that when usage was part of the name, the WALL-2-W Block was called B211-4W-TIE.

The rear building is comprised of WALL-2-W, WALL-3-W, WALL-5-W, and WALL-5H-W Blocks with WALL-1-W and WALL-1H-W Blocks filling the vacant notch locations. The left wall of the building is tied to the left low wall by a single WALL-2-W Block. This is the WALL-2-W Block above the top rear WALL-7-W Block in the low wall. Hidden behind the tie block in the building is another

WALL-2-W Block, which acts as a filler to complete that wall course. Abutting long Wall Blocks can therefore be tied above, below, or at the sides. Unwanted openings can usually be filled with combinations of WALL-1, WALL-1H, WALL-2, and WALL-2H Blocks. The ability to fill gaps is an important use for these short blocks. For small buildings, the WALL-2 Block is rarely necessary, but once a grid is breached, it becomes essential. At the right front of the building, a low, one-unit-long garden wall is tied by a WALL-2-W Block.

It was a few years before I discovered the full potential of the WALL-2 Block. As my buildings increased in complexity, I encountered more and more odd spaces that needed filling. No matter what the gap, I found that I could always fill it with the smaller blocks and I eventually arrived at the slogan: "I can fill anything." I don't remember exactly when or how it happened, but it somehow occurred to me that I'd inadvertently created a brick.

It's hard to imagine the capability unleashed by this discovery. The walls at the right and rear of FIGURE 4-01 are comprised solely of WALL-1-W, WALL-1H-W, WALL-2-W, and WALL-2H-W Blocks. In a sense, WALL-2 Blocks are the bricks and WALL-1 Blocks the mortar. Ungainly, but effective. Though it requires many more blocks, the construction of the right wall eliminates the need for the ties on the left wall. The brick concept highlights the importance of measuring blocks from their centers. Each course must align with the course above and below.

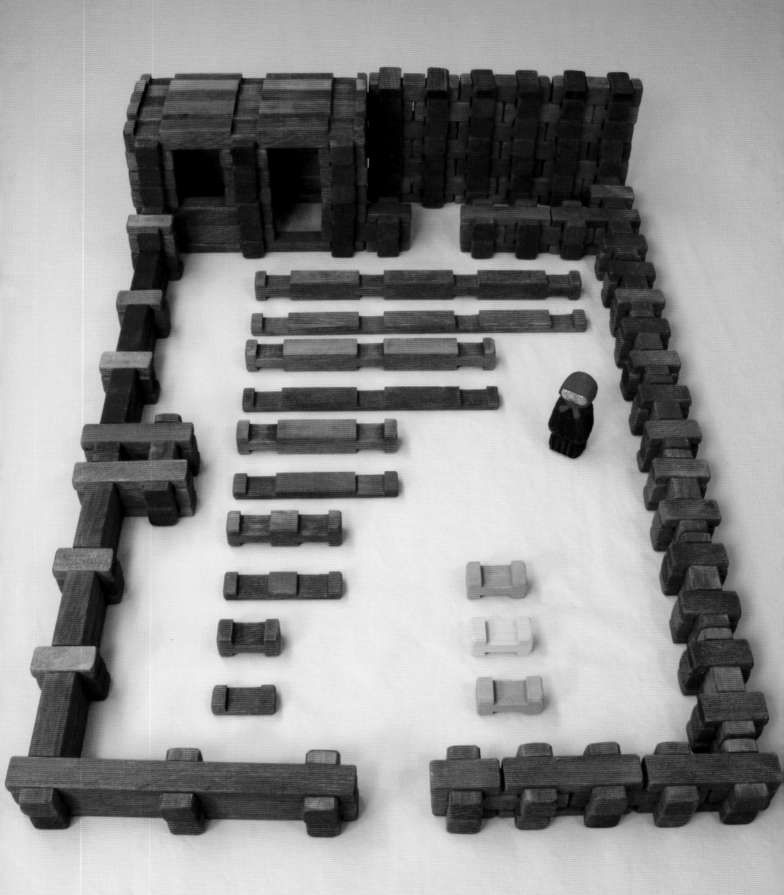

FIGURE 04-01: Wall Blocks

This figure also introduces a fundamental difference between the bricks and the blocks: **Orientation**. The walls in the front and rear begin with half sizes while those on the sides begin with full sizes. Both the front and side walls are two vertical units high, but the front wall consists of two half blocks and one full block, and the side walls consist of two full blocks. Orientation becomes more important as we progress.

For the smaller displays, I've included a Bill of Materials to give an idea of what's required for various constructions. The Bill of Materials normally excludes any loose blocks. Although the constructions are very simple, they show that a lot of blocks are needed to make anything substantial. They also give a good idea of the ratio of one type to another. WALL-1 Blocks far outnumber all other types, and the quantity of longer blocks is miniscule compared to that of the small, filler types.

FIG. 04-01 BILL OF MATERIALS

COUNT	TYPE
121	WALL-1-W
48	WALL-1H-W
42	WALL-2-W
15	WALL-2H-W
9	WALL-3-W
8	WALL-5-W
4	WALL-5H-W
4	WALL-7-W
251	TOTAL

In **FIGURE 04-02**, Rolfo relaxes in a garden scene.

The garden, including the arch, is comprised entirely of WALL-1, WALL-1H, WALL-2 and WALL-2H Blocks. A primitive step and a pair of benches are at the upper left. In the foreground, beginning at the left and proceeding clockwise, is the construction for a crossed wall. The first course ties the wall to the left, the second ties the wall to the rear, the third ties the wall to the right, and the fourth ties the wall to the front. The cross and partial cross in the garden are made in this manner. By using the smaller blocks, walls can be joined in four directions anywhere. If simple sheets of cardboard are acceptable for flat roofs, only four block types are required to make a building.

The shrubs are cut from kitchen sponges dyed green, and the grass is a large sheet of construction paper. The sponges, while stylized, are elemental and touchable, thereby satisfying those rules. If cut to unit and grid sizes, construction paper is reusable as well.

This figure also shows how colored blocks can enhance a model. The difficulty with colors is that wood colored blocks aren't of much use for a cement wall and clay colored blocks aren't of much use for a cabin. Color inherently violates the elemental rule. The Bill of Materials is just for the garden and excludes all the exterior blocks.

FIG. 04-02 BILL OF MATERIALS

COUNT	TYPE
64	WALL-1-CLY
8	WALL-1-SND
33	WALL-1H-CLY
7	WALL-1H-SND
23	WALL-2-CLY
1	WALL-2-SND
9	WALL-2H-CLY
145	TOTAL

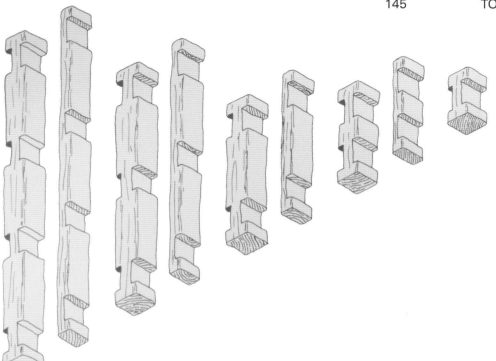

FIGURE 04-02: Garden scene and a crossed wall construction

FIGURE 04-03
WALL BLOCK DIMENSIONS

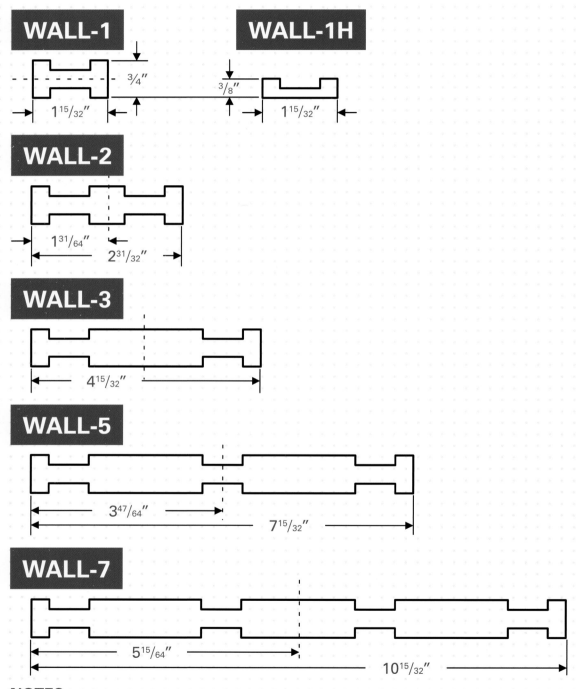

WALL-1　　**WALL-1H**

¾″　　³⁄₈″

1¹⁵⁄₃₂″　　1¹⁵⁄₃₂″

WALL-2

1³¹⁄₆₄″

2³¹⁄₃₂″

WALL-3

4¹⁵⁄₃₂″

WALL-5

3⁴⁷⁄₆₄″

7¹⁵⁄₃₂″

WALL-7

5¹⁵⁄₆₄″

10¹⁵⁄₃₂″

NOTES:

See FIGURE 03-03 for the complete WALL-1 Block dimensions.

Dimensions for the Wall Blocks above are labeled only the first time they appear.

For each Wall Block, there is a corresponding half Wall Block. Only the WALL-1H Block is shown.

CHAPTER FIVE

BEAM AND SPANNER BLOCKS

I didn't come up with Beam Blocks independently. They were needed because Wall Blocks didn't have sufficient notches to support the platforms and roofs that I was designing.

FIGURE 05-01: Beam Blocks

FIGURE 05-01 shows Hannah in a yard full of Beam Blocks; these are the same as Wall Blocks, but have an intermediate notch on one surface. They are three, five, and seven units long, and all lengths have half sizes. The beams introduced the duplicate naming conflict. Since WALL-1 and WALL-2 Blocks came earlier, there are no BEAM-1 or BEAM-2 Blocks.

The arched structure in the rear is the framework for a gable roof. It illustrates one use for beams — that of incrementally reducing or increasing the length of a wall. The base of the arch is five units wide. The WALL-2-W Blocks permit the centering of the doorway and also tie the low outside walls to the arch.

To the right of the arch is a pair of back-to-back BEAM-3-W Blocks. This construction shows how beams are used when all notch positions are needed both above and below. This always occurs with roofs as shown in the gable framework, and it often occurs in other constructions. If all notch positions are needed in a single course, I place two BEAM-3H Blocks back-to-back, but there's a better solution mentioned below.

The enclosure shows Beam Blocks used as fences. In one orientation, full beams are on the top course; in the other, half beams are on top. A two vertical unit high fence is thirty-six scale inches high, the height of a kitchen counter.

This figure also shows the emergence of the cement colored block. When I started with the blocks, I thought primarily of wooden structures. Once I thought of a base, however, cement blocks became dominant. Clay colored blocks arrived later when I found wood and cement alone too drab. The sand color came last, primarily as a highlight. The sand is a bit too bright for photographs when placed alongside other colors, so a slightly darker highlight might be better. The Bill of Materials excludes the loose blocks.

FIG. 05-01 BILL OF MATERIALS

COUNT	TYPE
2	BEAM-3-C
2	BEAM-3-W
2	BEAM-5-C
3	BEAM-5-W
2	BEAM-5H-C
2	BEAM-7-W
2	BEAM-7H-C
52	WALL-1-C
49	WALL-1-W
28	WALL-1H-C
6	WALL-1H-W
5	WALL-2-C
8	WALL-2-W
3	WALL-2H-C
166	TOTAL

FIGURE
05-02

BEAM AND SPANNER
BLOCK DIMENSIONS

Until I began writing this book, Spanner Blocks were merely a rejected idea. In three, five, and seven unit lengths, they could be considered a lazy type because they fit anywhere, even when not required. I chose beams over spanners to reduce the need for filler blocks and also because the beams worked well with my roof and wharf designs.

As the name suggests, Spanner Blocks would be most useful for bridging two grids and would therefore be one unit longer than the grid from which they project. The spanner would traverse one grid entirely for strength and then project one unit into the next. The next grid would usually be an unsupported overhang. Given three adjacent grids with the middle grid to be bridged, Spanner Blocks on each outside grid could support a cantilevered bridge over the center grid without other supports. This is a common construction, and, without spanners, a Rube Goldberg approach is required such as the back-to-back beams mentioned in a previous paragraph.

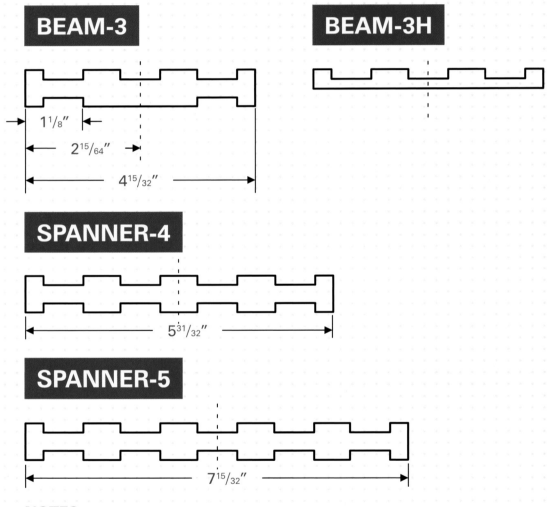

NOTES:

Dimensions for the Beam Blocks above are labeled only the first time they appear.

For each Beam Block, there is a corresponding half Beam Block.

Spanner Blocks are the same as Beam Blocks but with notches on both the top and bottom surfaces at each unit. They can be of any desired length.

LENGTHS:

BEAM-3 and BEAM-3H: 4 $^{15}/_{32}$"
BEAM-5 and BEAM-5H: 7 $^{15}/_{32}$"
BEAM-7 and BEAM-7H: 10 $^{15}/_{32}$"

FIGURE 05-02 shows a SPANNER-4 Block, six inches long, the very length I found useless at the start. I'm reluctantly introducing Spanner Blocks to the collection.

CHAPTER SIX
WALK BLOCKS

While the Wall Blocks were being stabilized and before I tackled roof construction, I thought of making platforms. Though I hadn't yet verbalized the thought, I was trying to duplicate bricks rather than logs. The platforms were to replace the green streets shown in FIGURE 01-07. I had no idea where I was going at this stage and wasn't particularly excited about the logs.

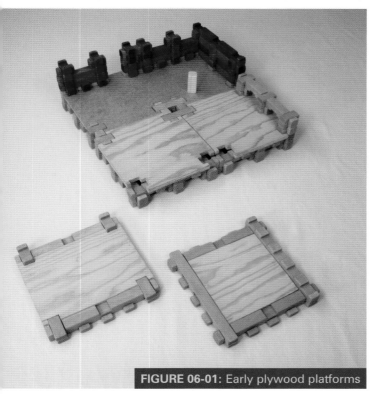

FIGURE 06-01: Early plywood platforms

FIGURE 06-01 shows the early platforms made of 3/8" thick plywood. Those in the rear and at the left have notches to accept blocks for walls and fences while the platform at the lower right must be surrounded by a framework for lateral support.

The construction in the rear consists of four square platforms. I made the two notched Masonite panels just for the example since I never made more than the two notched plywood squares shown here. A single notched platform posed no problem as a surface, but when I tried to place four together to make a large surface (as shown in the example) I was left with a hole in the middle. My first thought was to fill it with a plug as shown, but I quickly envisioned an endless collection of plugs in various lengths. My next thought was to

fatten one side of the WALL-2-C Blocks to fill the hole. Somehow, almost instantaneously, I thought of fattening an entire Wall Block, and the blocks hobby was born.

The discovery of the Walk Block secured the blocks as my hobby. Though I had made a WALL-2 Block the very first evening of the first session, it was long after the Walk Block discovery that I realized what I had in the WALL-2 Block. These two types are the essence of the blocks.

FIGURE 06-02 shows Oskar overlooking the collection of Walk Blocks. Though similar to Wall Blocks, the Walk Blocks are a full unit wide. However, while orientation is a curiosity with Wall Blocks, it is a major consideration with Walk Blocks.

The angled construction at the middle left shows that two variations of Walk Blocks are required to make a smooth corner. I call the two wall directions the **"A" orientation and the "B" orientation**. The "A" orientation Walk Blocks are the full width throughout and are in the left column of the collection. The "B" orientation blocks are narrow at the ends to accept an "A" orientation block and are in the right column. In the angled construction, the first course consists of a WALL-1H-C Block and a WALK-3BH-C Block. The second course consists of a WALK-1A-CLY Block and a WALK-3A-CLY Block. The third partially completed course consists of a WALK-3B-C Block. The "A" and "B" orientation information is part of the block name.

Unlike the Wall and Beam Blocks, some of the Walk Block lengths don't include half sizes. If "B" orientation Walk Blocks are always used as the first course on the sides of a display, there's rarely a need for half vertical unit "A" orientation Walk Blocks. A full vertical unit "A" orientation Walk Block in the front or back will always fit over the half vertical unit "B" orientation block on the side. Also, there's no WALK-5B Block as I've rarely found a use for one. For most block types, I make only those lengths and half height lengths for which I find a use.

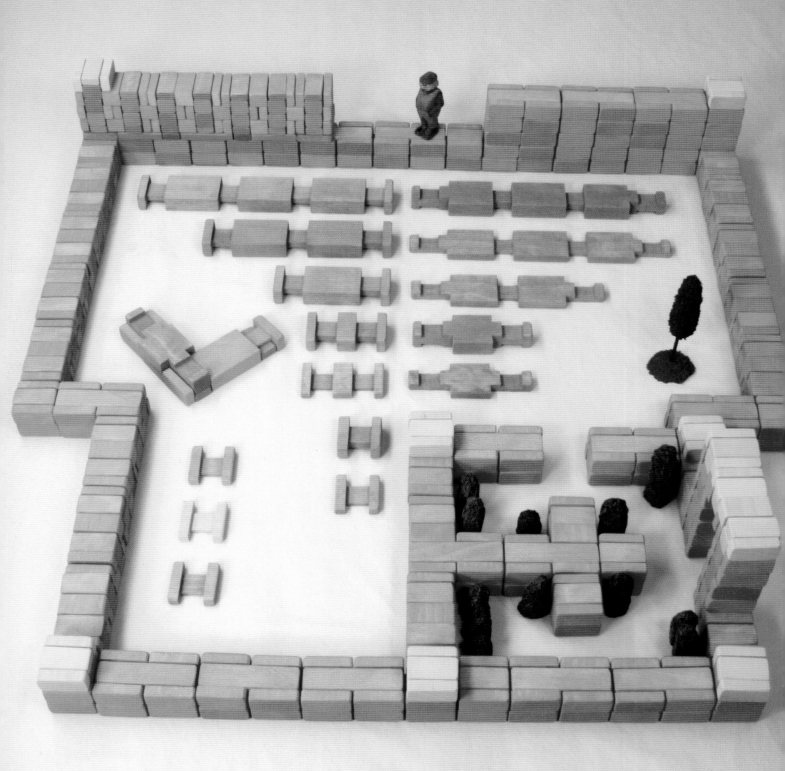

FIGURE 06-02: Walk Blocks

The high wall to the left of Oskar shows the difference in appearance between walls in the two orientations. In the lower part, the ends of WALK-1A-CLY Blocks are visible. In the upper part, the sides of WALK-2A-CLY and WALK-1A-CLY Blocks are visible as well as the ends of WALL-1-CLY and WALL-1H-CLY Blocks. The pencil-like line dividing the walls is comprised of a WALK-7BH-C, two WALK-1AH-C, and two WALL-1H-C Blocks. The cement colored blocks are not interlocked with the walls above and below.

At the lower right is a little garden similar to the one in FIGURE 04-02, but it's comprised of Walk and Wall Blocks together in order to make smooth walls. The construction of the cross is the same as in FIGURE 04-02, but both Wall and Walk Blocks are used.

The WALK-1AH and WALK-2AH Blocks at the lower left of the enclosure are often used as the bottom step in a stairway. The primitive wooden step at the upper left of FIGURE 04-02 would be vastly improved by a WALK-1AH-C Block. Also, I don't have any WALK-1AH-W Blocks, and a cement version would last longer.

While Walk Blocks in the "A" orientation are not particularly fragile, they cannot be dropped, certainly not on a cement floor. I am quite careful and rarely drop a breakable block, though it has happened. Fortunately, blocks can be easily glued with carpenter's glue, so I have never lost a block in this manner. Save the chip! It could be argued that "A" orientation blocks slightly violate the touchable rule, but I guess nothing is absolute.

The tree at the right consists of a round base, a dowel, and a rounded block with a green paint/sawdust mixture as the covering. Paint seems to work as well as glue for this purpose. It holds together, and the stylized tree is reusable.

As with the Wall Blocks, the WALK-1A Block is by far the most common Walk Block. They're small, so they should be made in the same manner as the WALL-1 Blocks.

Blocks in the "A" orientation are used much more than those in the "B" orientation, but when the Bs are needed, they are needed. The Bill of Materials excludes the loose center pieces.

FIG. 06-02 BILL OF MATERIALS

COUNT	TYPE
117	WALK-1A-CLY
8	WALK-1A-SND
2	WALK-1AH-C
50	WALK-2A-CLY
1	WALK-2A-SND
1	WALK-7BH-C
73	WALL-1-CLY
3	WALL-1-SND
2	WALL-1H-CLY
10	WALL-1H-SND
30	WALL-2-CLY
40	WALL-2H-CLY
337	TOTAL

The end units in "B" orientation blocks are narrow like the Wall Blocks in order to interlock with the ends of "A" orientation Walk Blocks, but the center units are the full Walk Block width (as shown in FIGURE 06-02) and the center notches mate with Wall or Beam Blocks. Walk Blocks can be made in the same lengths, heights, and half heights as Wall Blocks, but I haven't yet made all the possible sizes. I just recently made my first WALK-3AH-C Block, which is handy as a wide bottom step.

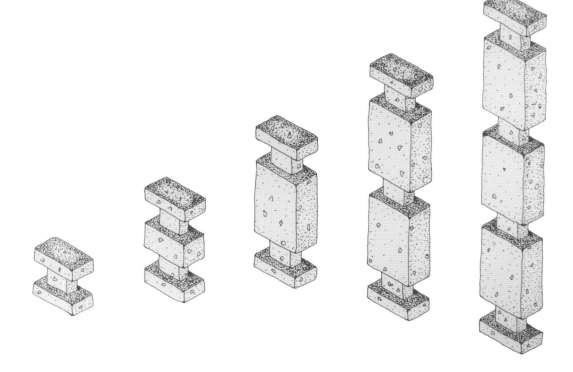

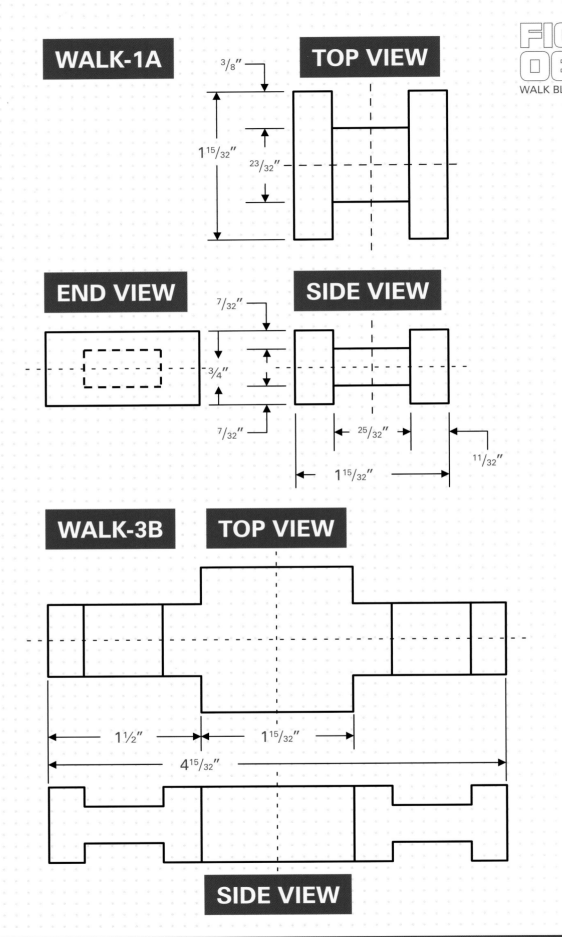

FIGURE
06-03
WALK BLOCK DIMENSIONS

WALK-1A

TOP VIEW

3/8"

1 15/32"

23/32"

END VIEW

SIDE VIEW

7/32"

3/4"

7/32"

25/32"

11/32"

1 15/32"

WALK-3B

TOP VIEW

1 1/2"

1 15/32"

4 15/32"

SIDE VIEW

THE STANDARD GRID CONSTRUCTION

FIGURES 06-04 through 06-09 show the construction of what I call a **Standard Grid**, which is a wharf with the area of one grid — 7 by 7 units — and is 2-1/2 vertical units high. This is the minimum height that allows water to pass underneath in both orientations. The foundations of all large block constructions are made up of standard grids, smaller grids, or extensions. Standard grids are the essence of bases. The notion of a wharf comes from the bricks as in Figure 01-07.

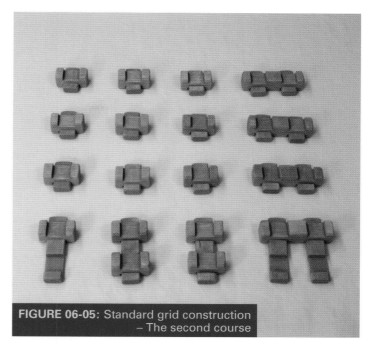

FIGURE 06-05: Standard grid construction – The second course

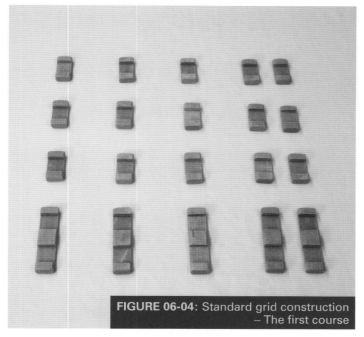

FIGURE 06-04: Standard grid construction – The first course

FIGURE 06-04: The first course

The left and rear edges will become edges of the wharf, and the right and front edges will be extended to other grids. The WALL-2H-C Blocks, which will tie the grid in front, are in place.

FIGURE 06-05: The second course

The WALL-2-C Blocks, which will tie the grid to the right, are in place. The mini-construction at the lower right would become a square if the adjacent grids were built. Two courses is the minimum required to complete this little square construction. If a base higher than the minimum 2-1/2 vertical units is desired, courses one and two can be alternated up to the desired wharf height. However, if the base will be very high, I normally make a perimeter framework at the minimum height and then make a full framework at the upper height.

A construction rule begins to apply here: **Always be tying.** When I was a boy, I used to visit a farm in Vermont. One summer when the annual wood supply arrived, I offered to stack it. I was enjoying myself, mindlessly stacking, when the entire pile suddenly collapsed around me. An old man who was staying at the farm saw my mess and introduced me to the tie. Continually through the pile, I was to shove a log halfway into the previous stack. "These are ties," he said. I remembered this when we had our own wood pile, and I apply it religiously for the blocks. Whenever two walls abut or sit side-by-side, I tie them continuously as they rise. Tying keeps the construction sturdy and also helps resolve the unevenness between block heights. My 3/4" block thickness isn't measured with calipers, and the old ones particularly tend to vary. Also, since I make large quantities of a single type in one session, and often make the type only once, a slight thickness difference may pervade an entire block type. I've thought of this problem, but the solution of using many boards to scatter the thicknesses runs afoul of the fun rule.

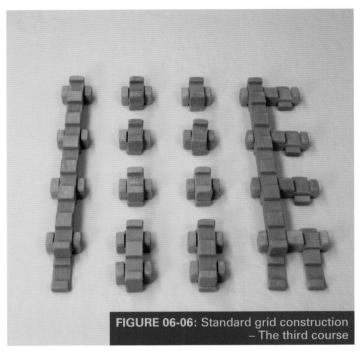

FIGURE 06-06: Standard grid construction – The third course

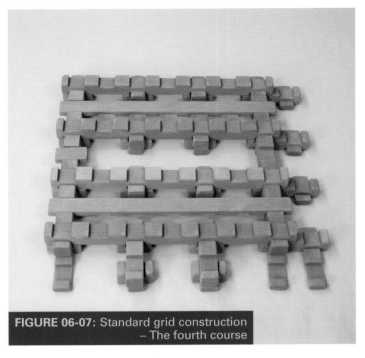

FIGURE 06-07: Standard grid construction – The fourth course

FIGURE 06-06: The third course

The left and right BEAM-7-C Blocks are in place. Water can pass underneath. Because Walk Blocks and their supports require all seven notches, Beam Blocks have seven notches on one surface. On the other surface, notches are required on only four units. It could be said that Beam Blocks function as logs on one surface and as bricks on the other. Blocks are very much the child of their two parents.

FIGURE 06-07: The fourth course

The four BEAM-7-C Blocks that support the Walk Blocks are in place along with two BEAM-7H-C Blocks, which are used to keep the Walk Blocks from rocking. For a visual display, the stabilizing half beams aren't necessary, but the wharf feels better with them in place. Water can pass underneath in both orientations. **I've arbitrarily chosen the first full block course as the "A" orientation of a display since it uses the WALK-A Block type.** In Figure 06-04, if a WALK-7A-C Block were to be placed on top of the WALL-2H-C Blocks, it would begin a flush wall along the front edge.

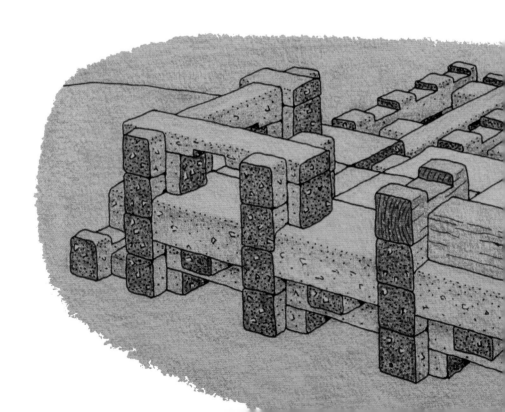

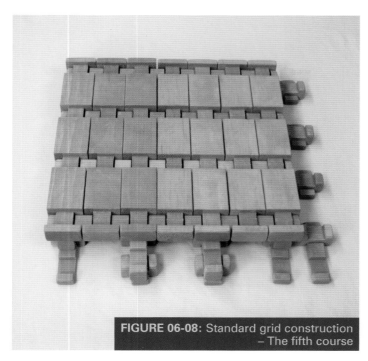

FIGURE 06-08: Standard grid construction – The fifth course

FIGURE 06-08: The fifth course

The Walk-7A-C Blocks are in place.

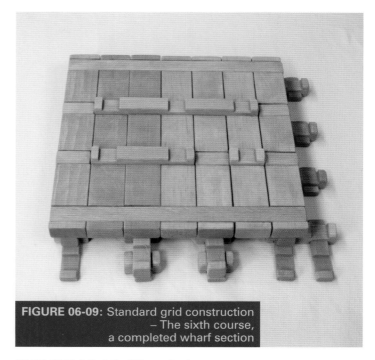

FIGURE 06-09: Standard grid construction – The sixth course, a completed wharf section

FIGURE 06-09: The sixth course

This completes a standard grid at the minimum height for a wharf. BEAM-1H-C and BEAM-7H-C Blocks are used to complete a flat surface, and WALL-1-C, BEAM-3-C, and BEAM-5-C Blocks are used as the foundation for a building to be erected above. The half beams and the structure base further tie the WALL-7A-C Block surface. Once I began making bases, I found that I needed cement colored blocks far more often than wood.

The ties to adjacent grids are clearly visible. In a full seven-unit grid, there are both center ties and end ties. In many constructions, particularly with castle walls outside the grid, ties are needed in two directions. In these cases, the centers can be used for tying in one direction and the ends can be used for tying in the other. Note: The Bill of Materials is for FIGURE 06-09 only.

FIG. 06-09 BILL OF MATERIALS

COUNT	TYPE
1	BEAM-3-C
1	BEAM-5-C
6	BEAM-7-C
4	BEAM-7H-C
7	WALK-7A-C
21	WALL-1-C
21	WALL-1H-C
6	WALL-2-C
5	WALL-2H-C
72	TOTAL

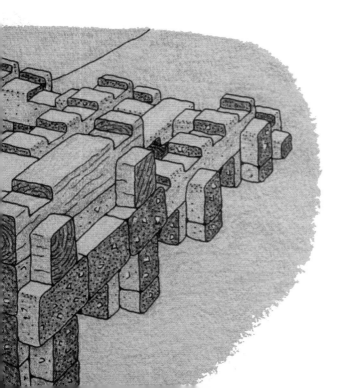

With the standard grid completed, FIGURE 06-10 shows Fulton rowing away from a fishing pier with a coot clearing the way.

The pier is a series of three adjacent grids and is one vertical unit higher than the standard height. Each grid is seven units long and three units wide, and one grid is offset. The walkways descending to the water show Walk Blocks used as steps. Each half of a vertical unit is a scale nine inches, about equal to a stair riser. The smallest area for a step is one-square unit as shown by the stairway in the middle corner. The half unit rise per step is accomplished by alternating the orientation of each successive course. The square stairway in the middle corner shows this progression. The orientation also alternates in each course for the more gradual stairway at the left.

The thinnest possible block interlocking is shown by the half vertical unit step at the bottom left. A massive mat could be made from WALL-1H, WALL-2H, WALK-1AH, and WALK-2AH Blocks, but I wouldn't be sure of its use. The simplest bollards are also shown, but they consume a lot of space and much more line than Fulton has room for in the rowboat.

FIG. 06-10 BILL OF MATERIALS

COUNT	TYPE
14	BEAM-3-C
9	BEAM-3-W
5	BEAM-3H-C
2	BEAM-7-C
4	BEAM-7-W
12	BEAM-7H-C
9	WALK-1A-C
3	WALK-1AH-C
6	WALK-2A-C
1	WALK-2AH-C
27	WALK-3A-C
1	WALK-7A-C
120	WALL-1-C
44	WALL-1-W
37	WALL-1H-C
18	WALL-1H-W
26	WALL-2-C
4	WALL-2-W
13	WALL-2H-C
355	TOTAL

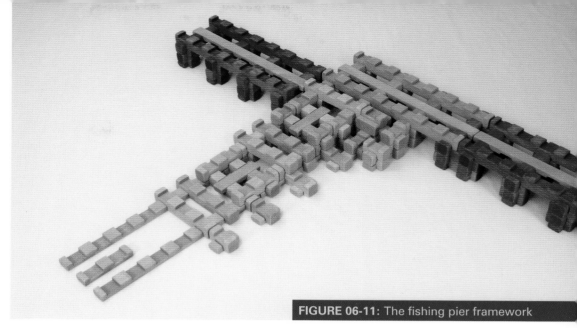

FIGURE 06-11: The fishing pier framework

FIGURE 06-12: The fishing pier step detail

The pier deck runs crosswise with WALK-3A-C Blocks, and each deck grid is supported by two BEAM-7-C or BEAM-7-W Blocks and a single stabilizing BEAM-7H-C Block. WALK-3A Blocks are the shortest Walk Blocks that can have a stabilizing beam in the middle. Two unit-long Walk Block grids can be stabilized somewhat by BEAM-2H Blocks above as shown in the third and fifth rise of the longer stairway in FIGURE 06-10. One-unit Walk Blocks, such as those in the corner stairway, cannot be stabilized, and though visually okay, they're always wobbly when touched.

The WALK-7A-C Block adjacent to the rowboat in FIGURE 06-10 is not tied to the stairway from below in the closer two-notch positions because BEAM-3-C Blocks underneath the stairway consume the only available notches to support the stairway. Therefore, the only tie from the WALK-7A-C Block to the stairway in the closer two-notch positions is the WALL-2H-C Block on top of the closest notch.

BEAM-7H Blocks can be used to tie large areas where there's not enough height available for a shorter tie. The two BEAM-7H-C Blocks at the lower left of FIGURE 06-11 connect the first two rises of the long stairway to the third rise. The BEAM-7H-C Block in the middle foreground of FIGURE 06-12 continues tying the longer stairway to the pier, and the BEAM-3H-C Block in the right foreground ties the small square stairway in one of its orientations to the pier. Once the rise is high enough, WALL-2-C Blocks alternate to tie the works together as shown above the BEAM-7H-C Block in the center of FIGURE 06-12. I removed blocks where the notch gaps are so that the BEAM-7H-C Block could be seen.

In conclusion, Walk Blocks can be used for flat roofs, floors, steps, streets, and walkways, as well as for piers. If doors, windows, and gable roofs aren't desired, and mosquitoes aren't a problem, Wall, Beam, and Walk Blocks can complete the collection.

CHAPTER SEVEN
ROOF BLOCKS

Since I like to include terraces on my buildings, the gable roof wasn't an early priority, but part of my reluctance to tackle the gable roof was the lack of a suitable precedent. The roof in my American Log set was a pair of isosceles triangle panels for the gables and a number of wooden slats for the roof. Only one length was included. Some log sets at the time had a series of diminishing log sizes to make the gable, but mine did not. I've seen a recent Lincoln Log set with a pre-cast plastic roof. The roofs for American Plastic Bricks were simply sheets of colored cardboard to be bent in the middle, but they did come in a number of sizes. All of these failed the elemental rule. The American Plastic Brick set did have gable bricks, but these were primarily intended to support the ends of cardboard roofs. I did occasionally use them for complete roofs, and Figure 01-08 shows a partial example at the upper left.

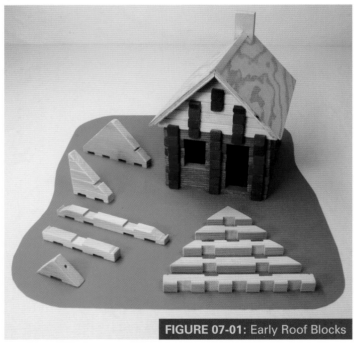

FIGURE 07-01: Early Roof Blocks

FIGURE 07-01 shows some examples of my early attempts at a gable roof, all of which were copies from the logs or bricks. The completed roof at the upper right is supported by gables like those laid out at the lower right. The roof itself consists of plywood panels that hook into notches in the bottom gable pieces. The ridgepole is an aluminum angle. If stained, this would be attractive, but plywood is very splintery and many sizes would be needed. I remember making a hinged

plywood roof, but I didn't save it when the hinges found a better use.

The gable peak at the lower left has a hole on each side. At one point, I thought of inserting pins through the roof pieces and into the gable in order to avoid the notched gable log. Above it are a couple of notch experiments, and at the top are two attempts at panels as gables.

In the very first log session, I discovered that logs are heavy and that they tend to stay in place even without notches. Years later, with this thought and the American Plastic Bricks gable in mind, I wondered if the roofs could be blocks. I often notice that if I ask myself a question, I get myself an answer, but until I ask a question, nothing is the answer. Once I thought of the roof as a heavy block, a design emerged.

The roof parts consist of sides and caps, each in two sizes so that the blocks above would overlap the spaces below. The half unit overhang at each end adds one unit to the length of a building. The roof pieces, therefore, are either two or four units long. In this design, I tried to keep the wall portion in the wood color, so the roofs became the first — and only — multi-colored block. The notched portion was stained, but the slate portion was painted. The color boundary — being awkward to paint — violated the fun rule and was soon dropped. I don't remember what the hole in the closest block was for. I used a lot of scrap lumber for the early blocks, and this may have been one of those cases.

FIGURE 07-02: The penultimate roof design

Each roof section has notches to interlock with the longitudinal Wall Block below, but the Wall Block is supported only at its ends by the gable. Notches are loose fits and aren't intended to support a block. However, the notches in the middle of the longitudinal Wall Block must support the notches in the roof section, and this caused Roof Blocks in the middle of the roof to sag. This phenomenon prompted the introduction of the **shim**. The exposed WALL-7-W Block in FIGURE 07-02 has cardboard shims in its notches to bring its height up to that of a normal supporting block. Given the loose notch tolerances, shims are required whenever notches are used to support a block.

Apart from the two-color difficulty, I made two other changes for the final gable roof design. First, I omitted the notches and had the Roof Block simply sit on the Wall Block below. Roofs are quite heavy and are not inclined to move. The current roofs are one of the few block types that are not secured in both orientations. The second change was a bit more subtle. The penultimate roofs were 1-1/4 units wide, and for the final design, I increased the width to 1-1/2 units. I did this so that roofs without a bottom overhang would center themselves in the middle of a Wall Block below. With the earlier design, a gap was visible along the bottom roof edge.

FIGURE 07-03 shows Antoine, in front of a local market, admiring the collection of Roof Blocks.

The larger Roof Side Blocks on the right have a cutout for an overhang at the ends while the smaller blocks on the left are used primarily for odd sized gaps. The ROOF-SIDE-2-T Block in the middle foreground is the smallest side block with the overhang cutout. Smaller sizes would fall off the end of the supporting Wall Block. Each Roof Side Block size has a corresponding Roof Cap Block. The cutout is omitted in all Roof Cap Blocks. The groove through the base of all Roof Blocks is exactly

FIGURE 07-03: The current Roof Blocks

3/8" deep. A completed roof is shown at the rear with the same supporting gable framework as that in FIGURE 05-01. A CHIMNEY-1H-C Block is at the upper left. Loose blocks are omitted from the Bill of Materials.

FIG. 07-03 BILL OF MATERIALS

COUNT	TYPE
4	BEAM-3-W
4	BEAM-5-W
6	BEAM-7-W
1	CHIMNEY-1H-C
2	ROOF-CAP-4-T
8	ROOF-SIDE-2-T
8	ROOF-SIDE-4-T
120	WALL-1-W
8	WALL-1H-W
9	WALL-7-W
170	TOTAL

CONSTRUCTING A GABLE ROOF

FIGURE 07-04: The first and second courses

The first course is a pair of crosswise BEAM-7-W Blocks. The Beam Blocks allow the front and rear wall lengths to decrease by two units. The second course consists of two front-to-back WALL-7-W Blocks on the sides upon which rest the ROOF-SIDE Blocks and also ten WALL-1-W Blocks to fill the excess notches. This filling is the reason I chose Beam Blocks over Spanner Blocks; otherwise, the entire gable wall would have been cavities and fillings, like teeth. The bottommost transverse BEAM-7-W Blocks are not part of the roof construction, but they show another use for Beam Blocks. The back-to-back pair converts three pier notches to four wall notches. If I had possessed such a block, a single SPANNER-7-W Block would have worked here.

FIGURE 07-05: The third through sixth courses

The first set of ROOF-SIDE-2-T and ROOF-SIDE-4-T Blocks are in place. The next rise of the gable is also in place. It consists of back-to-back BEAM-5-W Blocks and also the same pattern of WALL-7-W and WALL-1-W Blocks as in the initial courses.

FIGURE 07-06: The seventh through tenth courses

This is the same pattern of blocks as FIGURE 07-05, but for the next gable rise.

FIGURE 07-07: The eleventh through fifteenth courses

All the roof sides are in place and the final WALL-7-W Block supported by WALL-1-W Blocks at the ends. Two ROOF-CAP-4-T Blocks would complete the roof which is the same roof as that in FIGURE 07-03. The Roof Side and Cap Block lengths alternate in order to make a more attractive pattern.

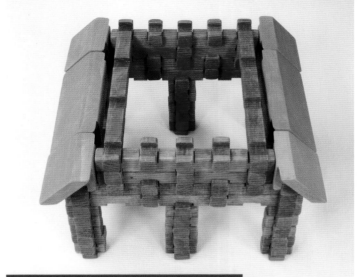

FIGURE 07-05: Gable roof construction, the third through sixth courses

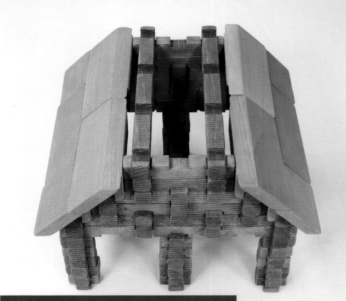

FIGURE 07-06: Gable roof construction, the seventh through tenth courses

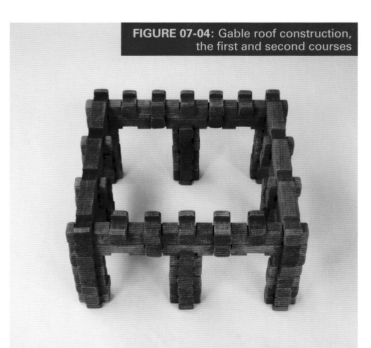

FIGURE 07-04: Gable roof construction, the first and second courses

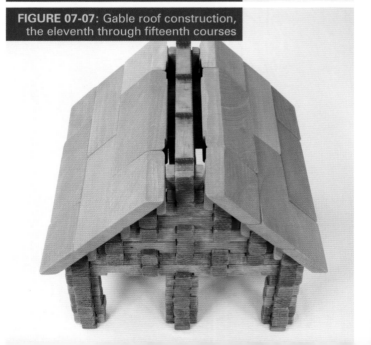

FIGURE 07-07: Gable roof construction, the eleventh through fifteenth courses

FIGURE 07-08
ROOF SIDE BLOCK DIMENSIONS

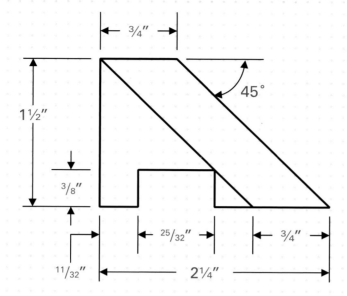

SIDE VIEW SHOWING INSIDE OF ROOF

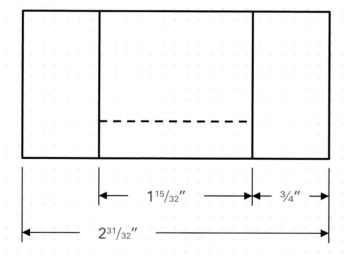

NOTES:

The 1-1/2" height, the 3/8" notch depth and the 45 degree angle should be as close to exact as possible in order for the Roof Blocks to mate properly. The other dimensions are approximate, and are intended to produce a loose fit with adjoining blocks.

LENGTHS:

ROOF-SIDE-.5: $^{23}/_{32}$" (no cutouts)
ROOF-SIDE-.75: $1^3/_{32}$" (no cutouts)
ROOF-SIDE-1: $1^{15}/_{32}$" (no cutouts)
ROOF-SIDE-1.25: $1^{27}/_{32}$" (no cutouts)
ROOF-SIDE-2: $2^{31}/_{32}$" (with overhang cutouts)
ROOF-SIDE-3: $4^{15}/_{32}$" (with overhang cutouts)
ROOF-SIDE-4: $5^{31}/_{32}$" (with cutouts)

FIGURE
07·09
ROOF CAP BLOCK DIMENSIONS

ROOF-CAP-2

END VIEW

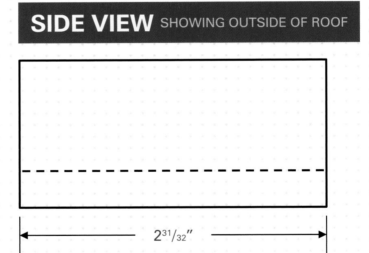

SIDE VIEW SHOWING OUTSIDE OF ROOF

$2^{31}/_{32}''$

NOTES:

The 1-1/2" height, the 3/8" notch depth and the 45 degree angle should be as close to exact as possible in order for the Roof Blocks and chimneys to mate properly. The other dimensions are approximate, and are intended to produce a loose fit with adjoining blocks.

There is no overhang cutout in any of the Roof Cap blocks.

LENGTHS:

ROOF-CAP-.5: $^{23}/_{32}''$ (no cutouts)
ROOF-CAP-.75: $1^{3}/_{32}''$ (no cutouts)
ROOF-CAP-1: $1^{15}/_{32}''$ (no cutouts)
ROOF-CAP-1.25: $1^{27}/_{32}''$ (no cutouts)
ROOF-CAP-2: $2^{31}/_{32}''$ (no cutouts)
ROOF-CAP-3: $4^{15}/_{32}''$ (no cutouts)
ROOF-CAP-4: $5^{31}/_{32}''$ (no cutouts)

FIGURE 07-10: Roof Dormer Blocks

FIGURE 07-10 BILL OF MATERIALS

COUNT	TYPE
21	BEAM-3-W
7	BEAM-5-W
12	BEAM-7-W
2	ROOF-CAP-2-T
1	ROOF-CAP-3-T
4	ROOF-CAP-4-T
2	ROOF-CAP-DORMER-1.75-T
1	ROOF-CAP-DORMAR-2.75-T
14	ROOF-SIDE-2-T
2	ROOF-SIDE-3-T
12	ROOF-SIDE-4-T
2	ROOF-SIDE-DORMER-1.75L-T
2	ROOF-SIDE-DORMER-1.75R-T
3	ROOF-SIDE-DORMER-2.75L-T
3	ROOF-SIDE-DORMER-2.74R-T
246	WALL-1-W
30	WALL-1H-W
18	WALL-2-W
5	WALL-3-W
3	WALL-5-W
15	WALL-7-W
405	TOTAL

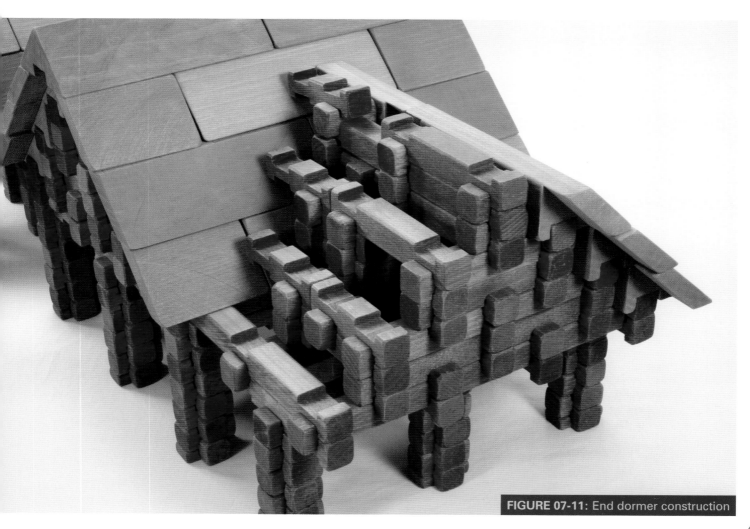

FIGURE 07-11: End dormer construction

FIGURE 07-12: Middle dormer construction

ROOF DORMER BLOCKS

Figure 07-10 shows Charlotte standing outside an open air market.

Roof Dormer Blocks rest on Wall Blocks in the opposite orientation from Roof Blocks, so they're a half vertical unit lower.

ROOF-CAP-DORMER Blocks come in three lengths and are like ROOF-CAP Blocks, but with one end cut at a forty-five degree angle. ROOF-SIDE-DORMER Blocks come in two lengths with left and right versions and are always made in pairs. The ROOF-SIDE-2.75L-T and ROOF-SIDE-2.75R-T Blocks have the overhang cutout on the square end, but the 1.75 versions are too short and do not have the cutout. The Bill of Materials excludes the loose blocks.

The eleventh course of the main building section consists of a transverse BEAM-7-W Block as shown in Figure 07-10. In this orientation, five vertical units provide a scale 7-1/2 feet clearance for Charlotte to get into the building. One vertical unit lower would allow only six feet. Ideally, this beam should continue to the right end of the building in order to support a longitudinal beam under the dormer, but I have no BEAM-11-W Block.

The beam support could have been continued to the right by using a BEAM-5-W Block in the ninth course, but Charlotte would have bumped her head. Instead, a BEAM-3-W Block is balanced on top of the end wall column in the eleventh course to support both inboard and outboard longitudinal BEAM-7-W Blocks for the dormer. The inboard longitudinal BEAM-7-W Block supports the framework for the portion of the dormer that's over the main roof. The outboard BEAM-7-W Block functions the same as the upper BEAM-7-W Block in Figure 05-01. Except for the portion over the main roof, the dormer framework is the same as that for the main roof. Over the gable itself, WALL-2-W blocks are leaned against the roof to loosely support the ROOF-DORMER-SIDE and ROOF-DORMER-CAP Blocks.

Back-to-back transverse BEAM-5-W Blocks span the gap between the two main roofs. These beams support a longitudinal BEAM-3-W Block, which, in turn, supports a column of four WALL-1-W Blocks. The WALL-1-W Blocks support a BEAM-3-W Block that lies between the main roofs to support the ROOF-CAP and ROOF-DORMER-CAP Blocks. This BEAM-3-W Block is balanced in the same manner as the BEAM-3-W Block mentioned in the side dormer dissection.

And, as the following construction steps show, with roofs as blocks rather than panels and with the variety of short lengths, a gable roof can be used almost anywhere.

FIGURE 07-13

ROOF DORMER BLOCK DIMENSIONS

ROOF-SIDE-DORMER-2.75-R

SIDE VIEW SHOWING INSIDE OF ROOF

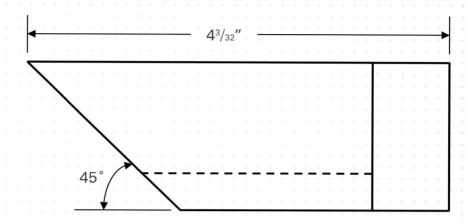

ROOF-SIDE-DORMER-2.75

SIDE VIEW SHOWING OUTSIDE OF ROOF

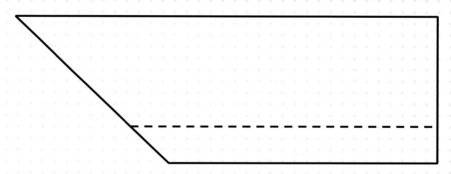

NOTES:

Dimensions for the Roof Blocks above are shown only the first time they appear.

The dormer sides are left and right pairs.

The dormer sides and dormer caps have the same dimensions as the corresponding Roof Side and Roof Cap Blocks, but are 3/8" shorter and have the 45 degree cut to fit against the roof.

The shorter Roof Side Dormer Blocks do not have the 3/4" overhang cutout, as they would tumble to the ground.

LENGTHS:

ROOF-SIDE-DORMER-1.75-L & R: $2^{19}/_{32}$" (no cutout)
ROOF-SIDE-DORMER-2.75-L & R: $4^{3}/_{32}$" (with overhang cutout)
ROOF-CAP-DORMER-1.75: $2^{19}/_{32}$" (no cutout)
ROOF-CAP-DORMER-2.75: $4^{3}/_{32}$" (no cutout)
ROOF-CAP-DORMER-3.75: $5^{19}/_{32}$" (no cutout)

CHAPTER EIGHT
HEADER AND FOOTER BLOCKS

The history of windows and doors is primarily the history of finding a way to contain them. Windows and their containment have been a problem since I began with the blocks, and even today I'm not sure my chosen design is best. More than with any block type so far, you may prefer a design other than the one I chose. One curiosity I have found with the blocks is that I often make all of a type only once. I then use it forever. If I think of a better design, as you'll see with the Footer Blocks, I'm stuck with the old design until I need more blocks. As with roofs, there was no satisfactory precedent with either the American Plastic Bricks or the American Logs. The bricks had elaborate window frames as shown in FIGURE 01-07, but no glass except for the jalousies. The American Logs had no windows at all.

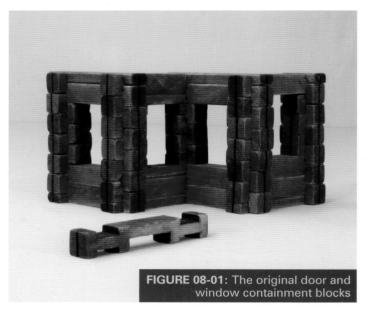

FIGURE 08-01: The original door and window containment blocks

FIGURE 08-02: Window containment from above and below

Not only is FIGURE 08-01 an example of my early attempts at constructing a window frame, but it also shows my first encounter with the orientation issue. The slots were designed to hold clear plastic sheets for the windows. The window height mismatch bothered me, and my first thought was to eliminate it. To accomplish this, I cut half a vertical unit from the middle of the blocks to be used in one orientation as shown on the left. The two window openings are at equal heights but at considerable cost. I soon surrendered to the orientation issue, and the unequal height of the right two openings has been the standard ever since. The loose block in the foreground is now hidden in a box labeled "Miscellaneous."

FIGURE 08-02 shows my early attempts at securing windows from both above and below. I thought first of a single header/footer design with a slot passing entirely through the block. However, a small window placed in the left opening would slip down through both the shorter footer and the longer footer beneath it. I thought of modifying the lower footer by notching it and adding an insert, but the mess at the right was the result. A thin paper shim would have accomplished the same thing. Looking back, I wonder what I was thinking. I now understand more about blocks and their behavior, and I hope my current errors are of a more sophisticated nature.

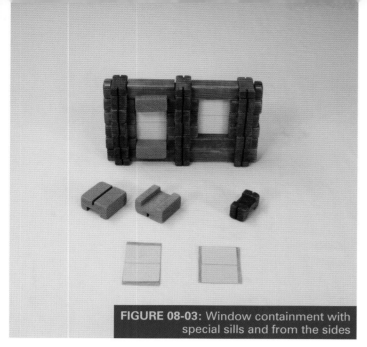

The window, shown on the right of FIGURE 08-03, is secured on the sides by the saber saw notches with a cardboard sheet representing the plastic. At the left is an attempt to make a header and sill as an insert in order to avoid special header and footer blocks, but the three-block vertical ensemble invited disaster.

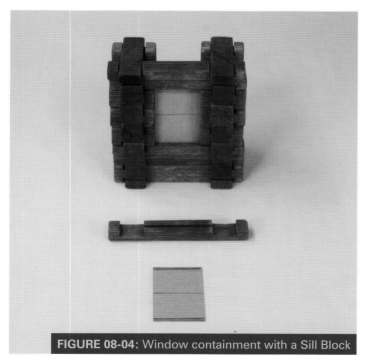

FIGURE 08-04: Window containment with a Sill Block

The blocks both above and below in FIGURE 08-04 would have a narrow slot to secure the window. However, aligning a window under the upper slot would be difficult, particularly with three windows in a row in a seven-unit block. A full depth slot in the upper block and a shallow slot in the lower block would provide the most secure yet easy to install framework. I have actually adopted this design in some of my newer windows. They're easy to install and very secure.

FIGURE 08-05: The current Header and Footer Blocks

In FIGURE 08-05, Sternwood gauges the merits of the current Header and Footer Block designs.

The Header and Footer Blocks are shown at the right and are the same except that Footer Blocks have a tab and Header Blocks do not. The slots go all the way through the blocks so that a window or door can slide through.

The construction at the upper right shows four HEADER-3-W Blocks ready to contain four windows in a tower. There is no bottom support for windows or doors. I use 1/8" thick plastic for windows and found the windows to be heavy enough that a bottom slot is not required. Window openings in one orientation are a half vertical unit higher than those in the other orientation.

The construction at the lower left shows the original Footer Blocks with a vestigial slot on one surface. Windows and doors were to fit in slots both above and below. Two Footer Block types were needed, one for each orientation. The tab on the Footer Block at the

FIGURE 08-06

HEADER, FOOTER, &
SILL BLOCK DIMENSIONS

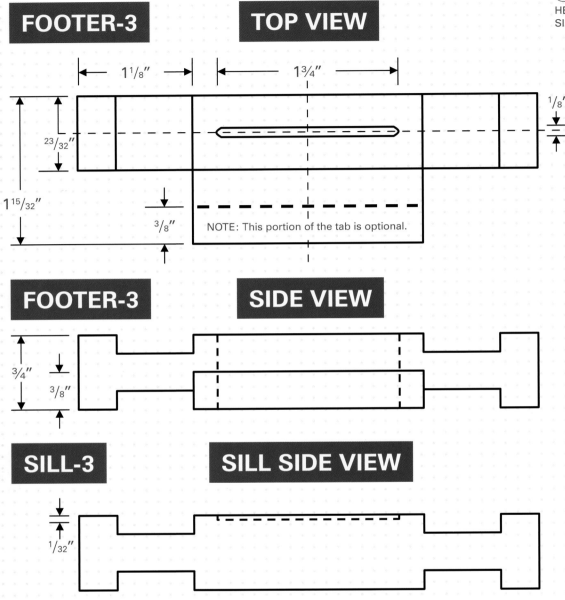

FOOTER-3   **TOP VIEW**

$1^{1}/_{8}''$ $1^{3}/_{4}''$ $1/_{8}''$

$23/_{32}''$

$1^{15}/_{32}''$

$3/_{8}''$ NOTE: This portion of the tab is optional.

FOOTER-3   **SIDE VIEW**

$3/_{4}''$
$3/_{8}''$

SILL-3   **SILL SIDE VIEW**

$1/_{32}''$

NOTES:

The dimensions for headers, footers and sills are the same as for Wall Blocks except for the addition of slots. The slot dimensions are measured from the center lines. Dimensions are shown only the first time they appear.

The headers and footers are the same except for the tab at the side of the footer.

The 1/8" slot width, the 3/4" block height, and the 3/8" tab height are exact dimensions. The others are approximate to allow mating with other blocks.

LENGTHS:
FOOTER-3, HEADER-3, SILL-3: $4^{15}/_{32}''$
FOOTER-5, HEADER-5, SILL-5: $7^{15}/_{32}''$
FOOTER-7, HEADER-7, SILL-7: $10^{15}/_{32}''$

FIGURE 08-06 also shows the dimensions for a possible Sill Block if a more secure framework for the bottom of windows and doors is desired. One surface of a Wall Block would suffice for this function, so no special blocks would be needed. A 1/32" slot depth is about all that's required. The early Footer Blocks in FIGURE 08-05 could also function as Sill Blocks.

right represented a 9"-high step that Sternwood used in order to get safely down to the base. The slotted half height block in the foreground would also have been a Footer Block, but without the step. When I discovered that windows and doors didn't require the bottom slot, I abandoned my original Footer Block idea. Doors now sit on the base in one orientation and on a half vertical unit high Wall Block in the other.

However, I found other uses for Footer Blocks and kept their name. The construction at the upper left shows FOOTER-3-W Blocks simultaneously acting as headers, Floor Block supports, bridges between grids, and window awnings. One of the middle FOOTER-3-W Blocks spans the two grids and points to another use for shims. A wood-colored cardboard shim is placed over the slot so that a 1/8" thick door set on the Footer Block won't slide through to the tenant below. I make a lot of roof patios, so this shim use is important. A thicker door would obviate the shim, but for some reason I didn't think of this until recently.

The wide tab makes Footer Blocks a bit unstable. It's easy to dump a load of windows onto the table during installation by accidentally tipping the Footer Block. Since the footer tab no longer functions as a step, it could be narrower and still support the floors. Footer Blocks would function perfectly and be more stable if the tab were 3/8" wide rather than 3/4" wide. The dimensional diagram (FIGURE 08-06) reflects this finding. Wide tab Footer Blocks actually violate the unit concept by extending into the next unit. If two narrow tab Footer Blocks had been used to span the grid gap, the result would have been the same as using a single wide tab Footer Block.

FIGURE 08-07 shows a window installed with a proposed SILL-3 Block underneath. The 1/32"slot depth shown in FIGURE 08-06 is adequate to secure the window. The current window muntin becomes 1/32" too low, but is barely noticeable. A Sill Block would be a Wall Block if viewed from the other surface. If a subset of Wall Blocks had a sill slot, no new blocks would be needed.

The original door design is shown at the right. The door is simply a thin board with penciled grooves. The knob is made of brass wire as shown in the white circle. The door slides through a HEADER-3-W Block and is not secured at the bottom. If a door is to be secured at the bottom, wall orientation must be considered.

The long angled wire is an **adjusting hook** that is used to pull windows and doors forward if they don't center properly when dropped through the slot. I slip the shorter end between the window or door and an adjacent Wall Block, and then twist the hook to grab the window or door from behind. This is an essential tool.

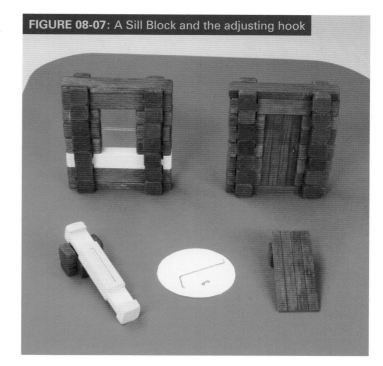

FIGURE 08-07: A Sill Block and the adjusting hook

In conclusion, Header and Footer Blocks are like Beam Blocks in that they're needed primarily to support another type. Without windows or doors to contain, headers are of limited use, and footers are needed primarily to support floors.

It's difficult to say whether doors and windows are best secured from the top only, from the top and bottom, or from the sides. I now have some of the second and third types, but I'm somewhat stuck with the top only method due to quantity. If you choose to secure windows from the sides, a saber saw or band saw would be needed rather than a router, and you'd have a box of notched walls rather than a box of headers. See Chapter 11 for the special Wall Block types required if you're using this method.

CHAPTER NINE

DOOR AND WINDOW BLOCKS

After the header and footer nightmare, windows and doors will seem anti-climactic. By the time it came to actually make a window, I had abandoned the thought of thin plastic. Sometime between the thought and the act, a partridge attempted to fly through our front storm door. Neither the partridge nor the pane survived. I took the insert to the hardware store and the fellow replaced the glass with thick plastic. He had a barrelful of scrap, but I saw little windows. This discovery led to the purchase of a router for containment slots, a router table, and a plastic blade for the radial arm saw. The plastic sheets are 3/32" thick and fit easily into 1/8" slots. They're also heavy and tend to remain in place without a bottom support.

FIGURE 09-01 shows Arthur, sitting in front of his retirement cottage, wondering what to do with the extra windows and doors.

The windows are one-unit wide and either two or three vertical units high plus 5/8" to fit inside the slot. The doors are also one-unit wide and are either four or five vertical units high plus 5/8" for the slot. The four vertical unit door equals six scale feet, and the five vertical unit door equals 6'9" with a transom above. The doorknob and the boards are scribed with a pen. The essential adjusting hook is shown in the white circle. It wasn't until I had nearly finished this book that I thought of making a thicker door like the freestanding one on the left. This door was made from the 1/4" thick scrap piece that results from re-sawing a 3/4" board to make a 3/8" board. The 1/4" thickness eliminates the need for a shim when the door is placed over the slot in a Footer Block. All my future doors will be of this thickness. It's amazing how long it often takes to think of something. Here, it never occurred to me to ask whether the shim could be dropped. The Bill of Materials excludes the loose blocks.

FIGURE 09-01: A retirement cottage

FIG. 09-01 BILL OF MATERIALS

COUNT	TYPE
2	BEAM-3-C
3	BEAM-3-W
4	BEAM-3H-C
2	BEAM-5-C
2	BEAM-5H-C
2	BEAM-7H-C
2	DOOR-5-W
1	HEADER-5-W
2	HEADER-7-W
1	ROOF-CAP-.5-T
1	ROOF-CAP-3-T
1	ROOF-CAP-4-T
1	ROOF-CAP-DORMER-3.75-T
4	ROOF-SIDE-2-T
6	ROOF-SIDE-4-T
1	ROOF-SIDE-DORMER-2.75L-T
1	ROOF-SIDE-DORMER-2.75R-T
6	WALK-1A-C
2	WALK-1AH-C
14	WALK-2A-C
1	WALK-2AH-C
2	WALK-3A-C
2	WALK-5A-C
3	WALK-7A-C
22	WALL-1-C
85	WALL-1-W
14	WALL-1H-C
4	WALL-1H-W
3	WALL-2-W
14	WALL-3-W
7	WALL-5-W
7	WALL-7-W
1	WINDOW-2-HM
4	WINDOW-3-HM
227	TOTAL

Arthur wanted a fireplace in his bedroom, so the chimney is located at the end of the building rather than in the middle. It's tied to the WALL-5-W Blocks with WALK-2A-C Blocks for most of its length. The cement-colored Wall and Beam Blocks of the base protrude into the wood-colored walls above. I arbitrarily chose to have the cement-colored blocks protrude into the wood to reduce the chance of any mythical water damage. With the orientation issue, color changes often involve a decision.

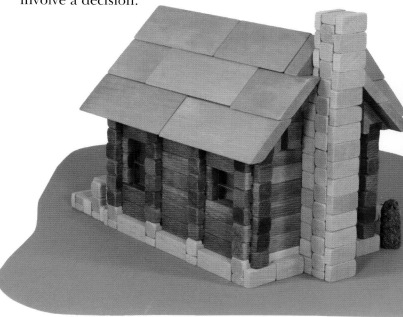

FIGURE 09-02: Rear view of the retirement cottage

In FIGURE 09-03, the BEAM-3H-C, BEAM-5H-C, and BEAM-7H-C Blocks tie the works together from front to rear. BEAM-7H Blocks are good for tying large, thin areas as was done in FIGURE 06-11.

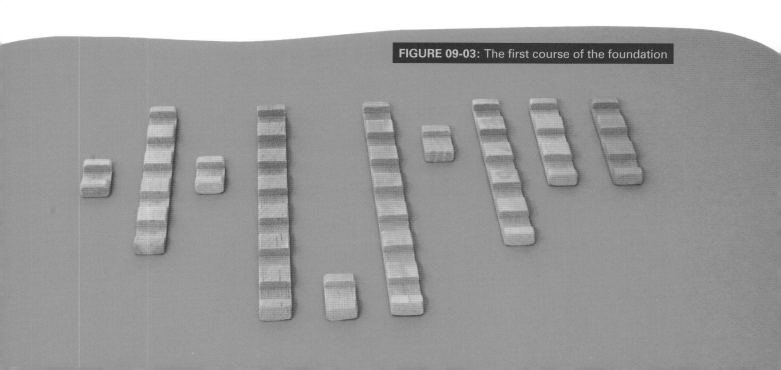

FIGURE 09-03: The first course of the foundation

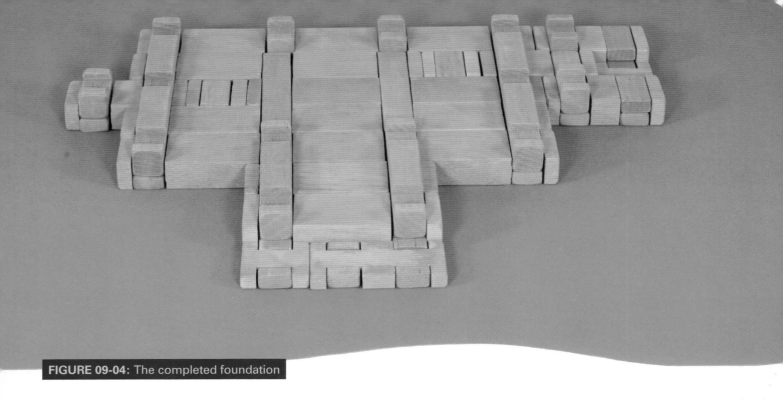

FIGURE 09-04: The completed foundation

FIGURE 09-04 shows the completed foundation. The two WALK-1A-C Blocks in the middle of the floor aren't tied to any other blocks, but are surrounded so they won't move. The protruding cement colored walls are in place.

In FIGURE 09-05, the WALK-2A-C Blocks of the chimney replace the WALL-1-W Blocks that would have been used had the chimney been in the center of the cottage. The shims lying along the longitudinal WALL-7-W Blocks help keep the Roof Side Blocks from leaning inward. Sometimes these are needed, sometimes not. The WALL-2-W Block in the top right foreground will lean against the gable roof. I have held it in place temporarily with tape underneath. The entryway is an open porch.

For the displays, which include a Bill of Materials, it may be helpful to gather all the pieces, build the structure, and then see if anything is left over, sort of like re-assembling a lawn mower and wondering what the extra washer was for.

FIGURE 09-05: The roof and chimney detail

WINDOW-2-HM

WINDOW-3-HM

FIGURE 09-06
DOOR & WINDOW
BLOCK DIMENSIONS

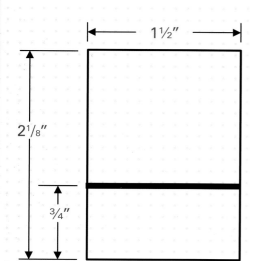

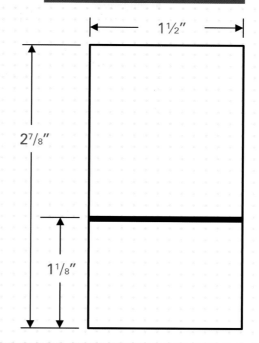

SIDE VIEW | FRONT VIEW | DOOR-5-W

DOOR-4-W ⅛" THICK

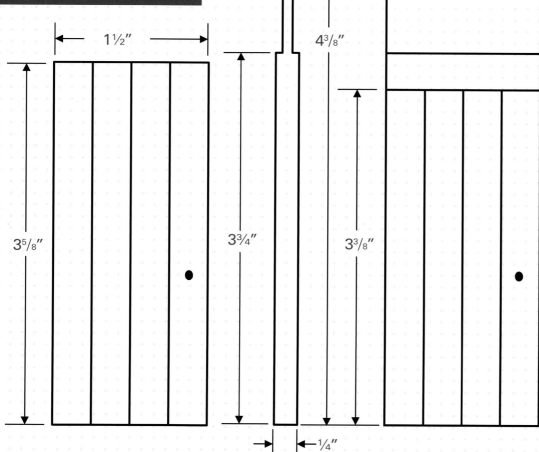

Plastic sheets 11" x 14" for the windows are found at the lumber mart. The plastic is hard to mark, so I do the measuring on the wooden stick shown in FIGURE 02-01 and use the stick to set the stops. Using the plastic blade, window-making with the radial arm saw actually satisfies the fun rule. Muntins are made with a partial cut.

The new doors are simply ¼" thick boards re-sawed on the table saw or on a band saw. I reduce the thickness of the top using the radial arm saw with the dado blades. With longer slots in the headers and footers, wider doors and windows could be used. For commercial buildings, these would probably look better. My wooden buildings look like something the Pilgrims might have constructed.

CHAPTER TEN
MAKING THE BLOCKS

Those of you whose vocation or hobby is woodworking can probably skip this chapter while the novices will probably wish it were longer. When I started with the blocks, I knew nothing about making small pieces, and I spent the first couple of years just learning how to handle them. Until I'd assembled the appropriate tools and learned how to use them, block-making was mainly a chore, but now I enjoy the making almost as much as the building. Both are now integral to the hobby. If you're just beginning with the hobby, the Wall Blocks used in FIGURE 04-02 would be a good place to start. Only four types are needed: WALL-1, WALL-1H, WALL-2, and WALL-2H. A single color, or none at all, will do.

All the blocks except for the windows are made using 3/4" thick clear pine. The widest board needed is 5 1/8", so nominal 1" x 6" boards, which are about 3/4" thick by 5-1/2" wide, are sufficient. I often get 1" x 12" boards because I sometimes make full grid sized blocks. Also, if you use a circular saw for ripping as described in Chapter 11, the wider board is easier to rip. Except for the windows, the first three steps in the block-making process are the same for all block types. The later steps vary and are discussed separately.

1. Select a clear pine board at the lumber mart as close to 3/4" thick as possible without being under. I bring a tape measure, and, without using the hook, check the thickness in a number of places. I find it embarrassing to spend so much time measuring and rejecting in public, but I continually remind myself of the haste penalty. Since I don't own a planer, I used to have a specialty shop re-saw a board for 3/8" and 1-1/2" thick blocks. However, for half thickness blocks, either the table saw or a band saw is sufficient for re-sawing, and I now laminate two 3/4" thick boards to make 1-1/2" thick blocks.

I accidentally discovered a problem with tape measures. The adjustable hook on the end may not stretch to the exact dimension. I originally used the hook for exact measuring but often checked a dimension with another ruler. I found that my cuts were consistently long and that the stretched hook was responsible.

2. Sand the board surfaces using a portable orbital sander, as shown in FIGURE 10-01. I use coarse sandpaper for this. If the board is very close to 3/4" thick, the sanding operation is more to remove shine than to shrink the dimension. If any quantity must be removed, use a fresh piece of sandpaper. I do almost all sanding against the grain to assist the staining operation and to stay away from fine woodworking. The fun rule applies here.

FIGURE 10-01: Sand the board surfaces

FIGURE 10-02: Cut the board to a convenient working length

3. Cut board to a convenient working length using the radial arm saw, as shown in FIGURE 10-02. I find that 24" to 30" is the longest length I enjoy ripping using the table saw. It's also about the longest length that's comfortable to cut using the radial arm saw.

For this cut, I support the far end of the board by tying a 2 x 4 that's the same height as the work table to a step-stool. For the initial convenience cut, I allow 1/8" extra — the blade width — for each block, plus an extra 1/4" as an allowance for error and to square the end of the board. The minimum ripping length on the table saw is about a foot, so the convenience cut shouldn't be too short. *Note: Cut just enough off one end of the initial board to square it and make the end smooth. This is done after the first convenience cut.*

After the convenience cut, three different processes are used to make the block types discussed so far. The Wall, Beam, Walk, Header, and Footer Blocks are all made in a similar manner and are discussed together. Roof Blocks require different steps and are discussed separately. Door and Window Blocks also require different steps and are discussed separately as well.

FIGURE 10-03
BLOCK MAKING ORDER - BY BLOCK TYPE

OPERATION	WALL-1 & 2 (using spacers)	WALL-1H & 2H (using spacers)	WALL-3, 5, & 7	WALL-3H, 5H, & 7H	BEAM-3 (using spacers)	BEAM-3H (using spacers)	BEAM-5 & 7	BEAM-5H & 7H	WALK-1A & 2A (using spacers)	WALK-1AH & 2AH (using spacers)	WALK-3A, 5A, & 7A	WALK-3B, 5B, & 7B	WALK-3BH, 5BH, & 7BH	HEADER-3, 5, & 7 (using spacers)	FOOTER-3, 5, & 7 (using spacers)
SELECT A 3/4" THICK BOARD	1	1	1	1	1	1	1	1	1	1	1	1	1	1	1
SAND BOARD SURFACES	2	2	2	2	2	2	2	2	2	2	2	2	2	2	2
CUT TO WORKING LENGTH	3	3	3	3	3	3	3	3	3	3	3	3	3	3	3
RIP TO 3/8" HEIGHT	-	4	-	4	-	4	-	4	-	5	-	-	5	-	-
RIP TO WORKING WIDTH	-	-	-	-	-	-	-	-	-	4	-	-	4	-	4
DADO GROOVES	-	-	-	-	-	-	-	-	-	-	-	-	-	-	5
RIP TO FINAL WIDTH	4	-	4	-	4	-	4	-	4	6	4	4	6	4	6
CUTOFF TO MULTIPLE LENGTHS	5	5	-	-	5	5	-	-	5	7	-	-	-	5	7
DADO NOTCHES	6	6	6	6	6	6	6	6	6	8	6	6	8	6	8
ROUT SLOTS	-	-	-	-	-	-	-	-	-	-	-	-	-	7	9
CUTOFF TO FINAL LENGTH	7	7	5	5	7	7	5	5	7	9	5	5	7	8	10
SAND TO FINAL WIDTH	-	8	-	7	-	8	-	7	-	-	-	-	-	-	-
SAND AND CLEAN	8	9	7	8	8	9	7	8	8	10	7	7	9	9	11
STAIN	9	10	8	9	9	10	8	9	9	11	8	8	10	10	12

NOTES: Those block types followed by "using spacers" means that spacer blocks are used in order to keep one's hands sufficiently away from the saw or router blade. All the blocks are made using 3/4" thick boards.

FIGURE 10-03 shows the operations needed for each block type and the order for performing them. The steps needed to make Wall, Beam, Walk, Header, and Footer Blocks are basically the same, but the number of steps and their order varies depending on the block type. The difference in operation order is for safety when a spacer of some sort is needed to keep one's hands away from the radial arm saw blade or the router bit.

FIGURE 10-04: Rip the board to the desired width.

MAKING WALL-1 & WALL-2 BLOCKS

1. Rip the 3/4" board to about 23/32" using the table saw; the board should be less than 3/4" wide.

FIGURE 10-05: Cut the shorter blocks to safe working lengths

2. Cut the board to the desired working length using the radial arm saw, as shown in FIGURE 10-05. Locate the stop on the side with your hand — which includes the block — so that the loose piece is free to move; otherwise, the cut may bind.

In the lower right corner of FIGURE 10-06 is a board cut to 9-1/2" in order to make one WALL-2 Block and four WALL-1 Blocks. The WALL-2 Block in the middle allows space for one's hands during the final cutoff operation. More WALL-1 Blocks could be made at the ends, and more WALL-2 Blocks could be made in the middle. If making only WALL-2 Blocks, at least two are needed for safety during the notch making operation.

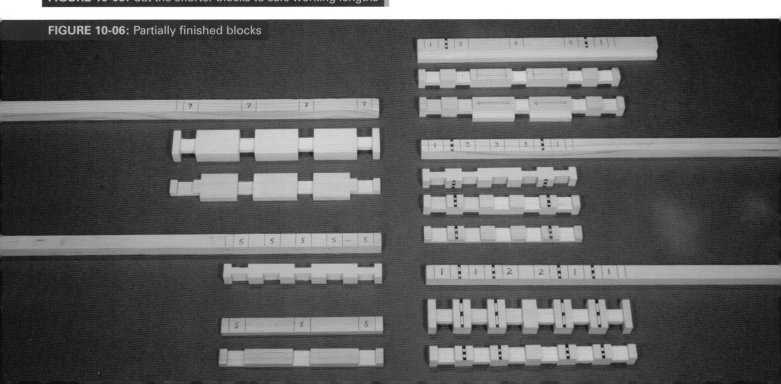

FIGURE 10-06: Partially finished blocks

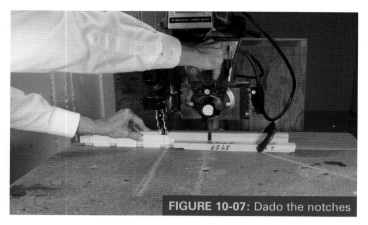

FIGURE 10-07: Dado the notches

3. Dado the notches to 25/32" wide and 7/32" deep using the radial arm saw, as shown in Figure **10-07.** The depth must be greater than 3/16". The photo shows a WALK-7B Block being notched, but the operation is the same. Locate the stop on the side away from your hand so that the block will stay in place. The dado blades remove a lot of material, so both the block and carriage must be held firmly. Notches at opposite ends of the board can be made with one setting. Check each setting before making a full cut to insure that all the notches fit reasonably well within the appropriate unit; otherwise, the blocks may bind.

4. Cut the blocks to the final lengths using the radial arm saw as shown in Figure **10-05.** Make the cuts from the ends toward the middle so that a WALL-2 Block is available for your hands during the final cut.

5. Touch both ends of each block to the belt sander to reduce the length to 1-15/32". The length must be less than 1-1/2".

6. Touch all the exterior corners to the belt sander to slightly round the edges, as shown in Figure **10-08.**

7. Clean the interior edges of the block with a sanding stick while holding the block over the meshed dust collector elbow.

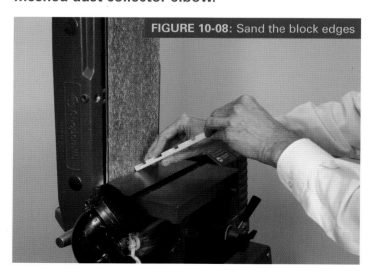

FIGURE 10-08: Sand the block edges

MAKING WALL-1H & WALL-2H BLOCKS

1. Rip the 3/8" height blocks from the edge of the 3/4" board using the table saw as in Figure **10-04.** Figure 10-04 shows a Wall Block being ripped, but the operation is the same. If possible, it's best to have the grain parallel to the surfaces of the block for strength, but it's not required. The grain on one by twelve inch boards is usually more parallel to the edge on the outside of the board than in the middle. This would put it more parallel to the surfaces of the cut off block.

2. Cut the boards to the desired working length, dado the notches, and cut the blocks to the final length in the same manner as is done for the WALL-1 and WALL-2 Blocks.

3. Sand one side of the block to 23/32" using the belt sander. The width must be less than 3/4". This step can be done before the final cutoff operation if desired.

4. Sand and clean each block in the same manner as is done for Wall Blocks.

MAKING WALL-3, WALL-5, & WALL-7 BLOCKS

1. Rip the 3/4" board to about 23/32", cut the blocks to the final lengths, and dado the notches to 25/32" wide and 7/32" deep in the same manner as is done for the WALL-1 and WALL-2 Blocks except that no spacer blocks are needed. The blocks can be cut to the final length before making the dado cuts.

2. Sand and clean each block in the same manner as is done for Wall Blocks.

MAKING WALL-3H, WALL-5H, & WALL-7H BLOCKS

1. Rip the 3/8" height blocks from the edge of the 3/4" board, cut the blocks to the final lengths, dado the notches to 25/32" wide and 7/32" deep, and sand one side of the block to 23/32" in the same manner as is done for the WALL-1H and WALL-2H Blocks except that no spacer blocks are needed. For WALL-7H Blocks particularly, be sure that the initial board is quite straight.

2. Sand and clean each block in the same manner as is done for Wall Blocks.

MAKING BEAM-3 & BEAM-3H BLOCKS

1. Make BEAM-3 Blocks in the same manner as WALL-1 and WALL-2 Blocks and the BEAM-3H Blocks in the same manner as WALL-1H and WALL-2H Blocks. BEAM-3 and BEAM-3H Blocks require spacer blocks due to the center notch rather than the short length. In the middle right of FIGURE 10-06 are boards cut to 7-3/4" in order to make one BEAM-3 and two WALL-1 Blocks or one BEAM-3H and two WALL-1H Blocks.

MAKING BEAM-5, BEAM-7, BEAM-5H, & BEAM-7H BLOCKS

1. Make BEAM-5 and BEAM-7 Blocks in the same manner as WALL-5 and WALL-7 Blocks and BEAM-5H and BEAM-7H Blocks in the same manner as WALL-5H and WALL-7H Blocks. For BEAM-7-C and BEAM-7H-C Blocks particularly, be sure that the initial board is quite straight. Once you're building bases and grids, these types become very important.

MAKING WALK-1A & WALK-2A BLOCKS

1. Rip the 3/4" board to about 1-15/32" using the table saw. The board should be less than 1-1/2" wide. If you don't have a table saw, the rip can be done using the radial arm saw without special hold down clamps, as the anti-kickback arm will work for this.

2. Cut the board to the desired working length using the radial arm saw as shown in FIGURE 10-05. In the lower right corner of FIGURE 10-06 just above the WALL-1 and WALL-2 Blocks is a board cut to 9-1/2" in order to make one WALK-2A Block and four WALK-1A Blocks.

3. Dado the top and bottom surfaces of the notches to 25/32" wide and 7/32" deep using the radial arm saw. The depth must be greater than 3/16".

4. Dado the sides of the notches to 25/32" wide and 3/8" deep using the radial arm saw as shown in FIGURE 10-07. Use a higher backstop than normal in order to accommodate the higher board.

FIGURE 10-07 shows a WALK-7B Block, but the operation is the same. The width of the final notch must be narrower than 3/4" so that a 25/32" notch will fit over it. This may take a pass or two to get right since it depends on the initial rip width. Since the block width is approximate, be careful when notching blocks that were ripped in different sessions that may have been ripped to a different width. This is a common problem.

5. Cut the blocks to the final lengths using the radial arm saw as shown in FIGURE 10-05.

6. Sand and clean each block in the same manner as is done for Wall Blocks.

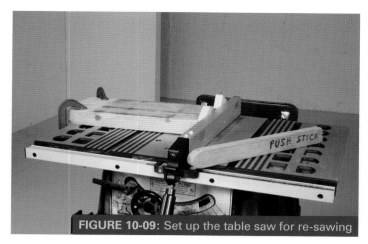
FIGURE 10-09: Set up the table saw for re-sawing

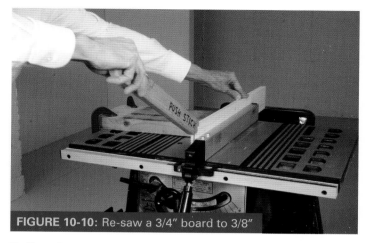
FIGURE 10-10: Re-saw a 3/4" board to 3/8"

MAKING WALK-1AH & WALK-2AH BLOCKS

1. **Rip the 3/4" board to 3-1/16" wide using the table saw in order to make side-by-side 1-15/32" blocks with a 1/8" gap between.**

2. **Set the rip fence 13/32" away from the blade on the right side of the table saw and set an auxiliary fence on the left side of the blade so that a 3/4" wide board will just slip through, as shown in FIGURE 10-09.** The table saw instructions show the auxiliary fence clamped at the front of the table, but I couldn't easily clamp it that way. Instead I used a scrap 2" x 8" board clamped on the left as the left guide. The extra 1/32" allows for sanding the saw marks from the final block. I used scrap pieces while setting the 3/4" width.

3. **Raise the saw blade to about 1-5/8" in order to rip a bit more than half way through the board.**

4. **Rip the board in two passes, as shown in FIGURE 10-10,** and use the push stick in the rear so that your hand doesn't fall into the blade.

5. **Sand the board to 3/8" and to remove the saw marks using the belt sander.** The board should not be thicker than 3/8". Save the remaining piece, as it's the correct thickness for making doors.

6. **Rip the 3/8" thick board to make two 1-15/32" wide boards using the table saw.**

7. **Cut the board to the desired working length using the radial arm saw.** A 9-1/2" length will make one WALK-2AH and four WALK-1AH Blocks.

8. **Dado the top and bottom surfaces of the notches to 25/32" wide and 7/32" deep using the radial arm saw.**

9. **Dado the sides of the notches to 25/32" wide and 3/8" deep using the radial arm saw.** The width of the final notch must be narrower than 3/4" so that a 25/32" notch will fit over it.

10. **Cut the blocks to the final lengths using the radial arm saw.** Cut from the ends toward the middle so that your hands will be well away from the blade.

MAKING WALK-3A, WALK-3B, WALK-5A, WALK-5B, WALK-7A, & WALK-7B BLOCKS

1. **Make the longer Walk Blocks in the same manner as the shorter Walk Blocks except that they're cut to the final length before the notches are dadoed.**

2. **Dado 1-17/32" from each side on the end units of the WALK-3B, WALK-5B, and WALK-7B Blocks as shown in FIGURE 10-07.** This allows the end of an "A" orientation Walk Block to interlock with the end of a "B" orientation block.

MAKING HEADER-3, HEADER-5, & HEADER-7 BLOCKS

NOTE: If you prefer to secure doors and windows from the sides rather than from the top, see Chapter 11.

1. Make Header Blocks in the same manner as BEAM-3 Blocks, but omit the extra center notch. Like BEAM-3 Blocks, all Header Blocks require a spacer block on each end due to the slots. At the top right of Figure 10-06 is a board cut to 10 3/4" in order to make one HEADER-5 and two WALL-1 Blocks.

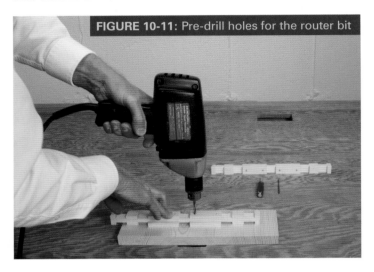

FIGURE 10-11: Pre-drill holes for the router bit

2. Drill 3/16" diameter pilot holes centered at the ends of each 1-1/2" slot using a portable drill, as shown in FIGURE 10-11. The pilot holes eliminate the jolt when the board encounters the router bit. A smaller pilot hole can be drilled first to help make the 3/16" hole more accurate. To the right of the drill are an awl and a smaller bit. If you have a drill press, this operation would be more accurate and also fun. My hand drilling isn't the best.

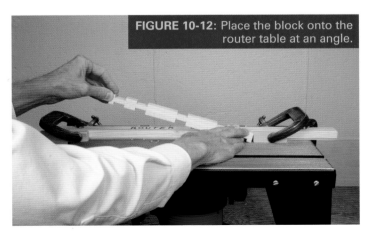

FIGURE 10-12: Place the block onto the router table at an angle.

3. Set up the router table for (one of) the slots, as shown in FIGURE 10-12. The backstop should be set so that the slot is centered on the block, and the side stops should allow the router bit to pass from one pilot hole to the other. A 1/8" diameter router bit with a 2" shank cuts only 3/8" deep, so with one stop setting, only half of a slot can be routed. For a HEADER-5 Block, half of one slot on one surface and half of the other slot on the other surface can be routed with one stop setting, then the side stop settings must be reversed to finish the slots.

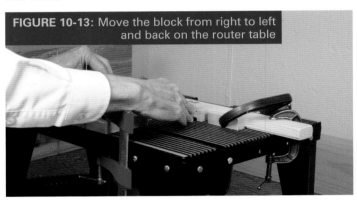

FIGURE 10-13: Move the block from right to left and back on the router table

4. Clamp a face guard between the router bit and the front of the table, as shown in FIGURE 10-13.

5. Press the Header Block against the backstop and the right side stop at an angle, as shown in FIGURE 10-12. The face guard is removed to show the placement. It's important to pass from right to left so that the router bit forces the block against the backstop.

6. Lower the block onto the router bit, pass the block from right to left, and then pass the block back to the right. Rout only 1/8" at a time to avoid straining the bit. This operation takes about four passes.

7. Lift the block up from the left while holding the right end to the backstop and the right side stop as shown in FIGURE 10-12. It's important to hold the block tightly so that the router bit won't become misaligned. Even with care, slight jolts occur. In the manner that I use them, the surfaces of Header and Footer Blocks are rarely exposed, so slight aberrations in the pilot holes, the centering, and the jolts aren't a problem. Although it's not my favorite, the routing operation isn't too bad if you're careful.

MAKING FOOTER-3, FOOTER-5, & FOOTER-7 BLOCKS

As with Header Blocks, if you prefer to secure doors and windows from the sides rather than from the top, see Chapter 11. However, Footer Blocks are also used to support floors, so they would still be made, but without the slots.

Footer Blocks are the same as Header Blocks except for the 3/8" tab. Most of my Footer Blocks have a 3/4" tab because they were made before I understood the unit concept, but there's no need for the extra 3/8".

1. Rip the 3/4" board to 2 5/16" using the table saw as shown in FIGURE **10-04,** which shows a Wall Block being ripped, but the operation is the same. This will make side-by-side pairs of 1-3/32" blocks with 1/8" remaining for a final rip to separate the blocks.

2. Dado a 7/8" wide and 3/8" deep groove along the center of the board using the radial arm saw, as shown in FIGURE **10-14.** With the 25/32" dado set, this requires two passes. The depth should be exactly 3/8" since blocks will rest on the surfaces.

3. Rip the board along the center using the table saw; this will make two 1-3/32" wide boards with the 3/8" tab.

4. Make the Footer Block notches and slots in the same manner as Header Blocks. Use spacer blocks in the same manner.

5. Dado the cutout portions of the tab using the radial arm saw as shown in FIGURES **08-05 and 08-06.** Note that the end cutouts in the tabs do not extend into the block a full unit. They do not accommodate the end of a Walk Block. The tab is removed entirely on the end spacer WALL-1 Blocks.

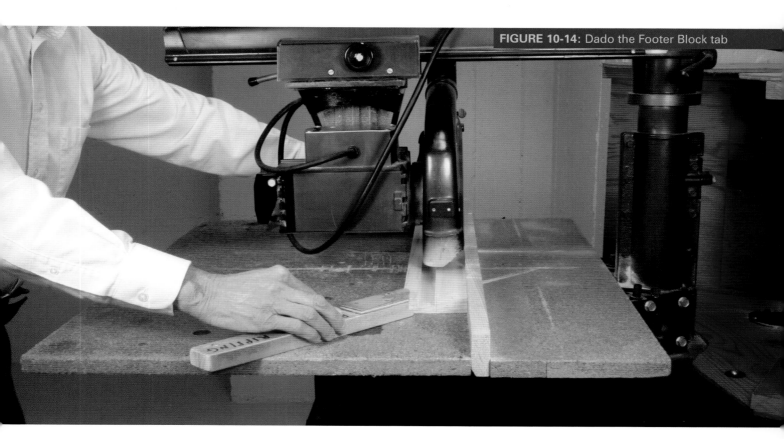

FIGURE 10-14: Dado the Footer Block tab

FIGURE 10-15

TEMPLATE FOR ROOF CAP
& ROOF SIDE BLOCKS

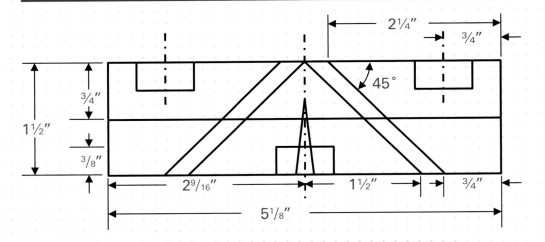

Template for ROOF-CAP & ROOF-SIDE Blocks

Template for ROOF-SIDE Blocks only

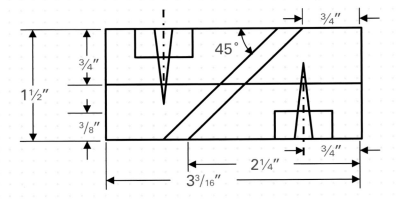

MAKING ROOF & ROOF DORMER BLOCKS

Roof Blocks require a 1-1/2" thick board. I made two templates as shown in FIGURE 10-15, one for making ROOF-SIDE and ROOF-CAP Blocks together, and one for making ROOF-SIDE Blocks alone. The templates determined the board width. For narrow gables, two sides for each cap will suffice, but for wider roofs, extra sides are needed.

NOTES:

For each lamination, a temporary flat head 1" #8 wood screw is used at each end to keep the pieces aligned during the gluing operation. Each screw is located about 2" from the end of the boards in order to keep the screw holes away from any overhang cutouts.

The large gap between the roof pieces allows for sanding the saw marks to make a smooth roof surface.

1. Rip two boards to either 3-3/16" or 5-1/8" wide using the table saw depending on which combination you're planning to make. These boards should be quite straight and compatible since they'll be laminated. For the example, I made a 5-1/8" lamination.

2. Screw the boards together in two places. If the screws are located as shown in the diagrams, they won't interfere with the slope or an end overhang. Errors led to this revelation.

3. Undo the screws.

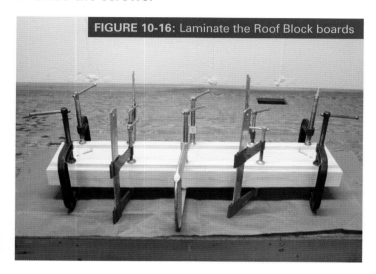
FIGURE 10-16: Laminate the Roof Block boards

4. Glue the boards together with carpenter's glue using the screws to align them as shown in FIGURE 10-16. I used some scrap wood to help distribute the pressure and reduce the clamp marks.

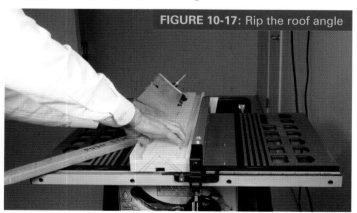
FIGURE 10-17: Rip the roof angle

5. Mark each end of the laminated board using the template as a guide; the marks help when positioning the saw blade.

6. Locate the table saw blade at a 45-degree angle between the marks. The wide gap between the marks allows for sawing anomalies and for removing the saw marks for a smooth roof.

7. Rip the first 45-degree angle using the table saw with the ROOF-CAP Block as shown. If it's reversed, the second cut is rather awkward. An error also led to this revelation. Be sure to use the push stick and the blade guard, and keep your right hand away from the cut.

8. Rip the second 45-degree angle. If the ROOF-CAP Block is located as shown, the second rip is the same as the first. If it's reversed, you're stuck with a knife edge for a guide.

FIGURE 10-18: Cut the dormer angle

9. Cut the 45-degree angles for any ROOF-CAP-DORMER and ROOF-SIDE-DORMER Blocks from the end of the stock using the radial arm saw. This is the easiest time to make these. One guide edge will be a knife edge. A dormer from each end of the side stock will result in a left/right pair. Be sure to clamp or stop the stock since 45-degree cuts tend to push the board laterally.

FIGURE 10-19: Dado the roof overhang

10. Dado the overhang cutouts using the radial arm saw. Make the ROOF-SIDE-2 Blocks in pairs for safety. See FIGURES 07-08, 07-09, and 07-13 to determine which block types have the overhang cutout.

11. Cut the roofs to the nominal length using the radial arm saw. Use any leftover stock to make the narrower caps and sides; however, there's usually very little scrap remaining.

12. Sand the roof slope to the final thickness using the belt sander; this also removes the saw marks.

13. Sand the inside vertical surface and the roof ends so that they're less than the nominal dimension. These surfaces abut adjacent blocks and must not bind. Round the edges a bit so they're not sharp, and clean the block.

MAKING DOOR BLOCKS

Door blocks can be made from the scrap remaining after a 3/4" board is re-sawed to make a 3/8" board. As long as the door will cover a 1/8" slot comfortably, the door is thick enough, though it can be thicker.

1. Rip the board to 1-1/2" using the table saw. For the doors and windows, I use the nominal dimensions so that the fits will be tighter in order to look better.

2. Cut the door to 1/8" less than the next greater vertical unit using the radial arm saw as shown in FIGURE 09-06. This is done so that the door won't poke the block above it. However, if you're securing the doors from the sides, the door will be wider rather than higher.

3. Dado the top to 1/8" thick using the radial arm saw so it'll fit into the Header Block slot.

4. Score the simulated boards and knobs with a black pen and a straight edge as desired, though you can make more complex doors with window openings if you'd like.

MAKING WINDOW BLOCKS

I make Window Blocks from 11" x 14" sheets of 3/32" thick plastic from the lumber mart. I bought a plastic cutting blade for this as shown on the lower right of FIGURE 02-01. This blade creates little curlicues and curlicue clumps rather than sawdust, and the curlicues are a bit clingy. The process also smells somewhat, so I use fans to circulate air from outside. Other than that, the cutting is easy and window-making is actually fun.

1. Plan the cuts on paper in advance in order to get as many windows as possible from one sheet. Some patterns yield more windows than others, and it's not easy to make a partial cut. I've never tried.

2. Locate the stop for one dimension using either a ruler or a stick like the ones shown on the right of FIGURE 02-01. The film covering the plastic sheet is hard to mark. Since the sheets are thin, I don't use the cutout end of the stops for this and I clear the backstop area with the dust collector after each cut.

3. Cut the sheet in one dimension using the radial arm saw with the plastic blade. I have no idea what would happen if a combination blade were used; I have never tested the notion. Be careful not to scratch the windows. Though they're not fragile, they also won't stand rough handling. I keep my windows separated by file cards in boxes.

4. Cut the window to the final length or width in the other dimension using the radial arm saw.

5. Cut the muntins in each window by making about a 1/32" deep pass. Any scratch renders the plastic translucent, so the cut needn't be deep.

6. Sand the edges as needed using a sanding stick to remove any flash that was generated by the saw; the windows are now finished.

STAINING THE BLOCKS

All the blocks other than the windows can be stained. I use a wood color, a cement color, a clay color, a sand color, and a tar color. One important fact I have learned through the years: *Save the formulas.*

Over the course of fifteen years, the brands and available stain colors have changed, so it's probably a good idea to select popular colors. I first bought Behr water-based stains, but Behr ultimately discontinued the line. Minwax® has some of the same colors that I started with, but some vary slightly. I haven't yet found a good solution to this problem, and there's absolutely no law that requires staining at all if you like the look and smell of bare wood.

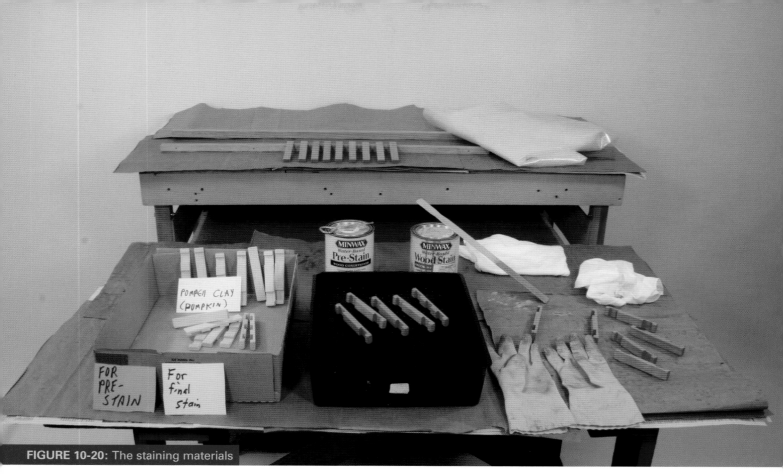

1. Set up your tools and their arrangement, as shown in FIGURE 10-20. I use water-based stains even though they're less stable than oil-based, but oil-based stains heavily violate the fun rule. I place a box of blocks on the left side of the staining table, a paint tray to stain and drain the blocks in the middle, and a cut-up paper bag over newsprint on the right side to further drain the stained blocks. In the rear I have a rag to wipe each tray load of blocks before moving the blocks to a drying table. On another table, I have many rows of scrap lumber on top of bags and newsprint upon which to lean the wiped blocks for drying. I use little cards like those on the left to label the steps and the colors. I make blocks in large quantities, and without the labels, I'd make many more staining errors than I do. Staining is permanent.

2. Sand and clean the blocks to the extent that you would like. As you can probably guess, the *fun rule* imposes some limits here.

3. Pre-stain the block using a water-based pre-stain. It's not necessary to wipe the blocks after this operation. Once they're drained, I place them onto the drying table.

4. If needed, lightly sand the top and bottom surfaces of the block using the belt sander. This is rarely required, but sometimes the grain rises as a result of the pre-stain operation.

5. Stain the block using a water-based stain. For the color stain, I do wipe the block before drying. One coat is sufficient, and I don't use anything to protect the finish.

CHAPTER ELEVEN

MAKING THE BLOCKS: ALTERNATIVE METHODS

Over the years, I have acquired the tools I need in order to make each operation enjoyable, but in the beginning, I suffered with the tools I had. This chapter discusses alternate ways for making the blocks if you don't have all the stationary power tools that I currently use.

The power tools that I currently use are an orbital sander, a radial arm saw, a table saw, a belt sander, a router, and a dust collector. When I began, however, I had only a radial arm saw, an orbital sander, a circular saw, and a saber saw. As I progressed, I purchased the dust collector, belt sander, table saw, and router in that order.

Much later, I bought a band saw, and I now use it for ripping boards to the 3/8" thickness. It's an expensive addition, so I didn't mention it in the previous chapter since the table saw works well for re-sawing. The band saw does make re-sawing fun, however. It's possible to make an entire block with the band saw, and for a single, complicated block, it's the easiest tool to use. I also bought a drill press in order to drill accurate holes. Like the band saw, it's not required, and also like the band saw, the drill press makes drilling fun rather than a chore.

RIPPING WITH A CIRCULAR SAW

If you don't have a table saw and don't want to rip narrow widths on the radial arm saw, you can use a portable circular saw with the guide. I used a circular saw until I bought the table saw. If you're using a circular saw, select a 1" x 12" board at the lumber mart like the one shown in Figure 10-01. Rip the 3/8" thick and 23/32" wide blocks first using the circular saw. For 3/8" thick blocks, rip the board a bit wider than 3/8" and then sand it to the final thickness using the belt sander. The 3/8" thick blocks will function okay if they're a bit less than 3/8", but they must not be over. The 23/32" wide blocks may be less accurate than what's possible with the table saw, but as long as the 23/32" width is less than 3/4", they'll be okay. When the board becomes too narrow for the guide, use the remainder of the board for the 1-3/32" and 1-15/32" wide blocks. The radial arm saw anti-kickback arm will work for these. One advantage of the circular saw is that it can be used outdoors to reduce dust if you don't have a dust collector.

It's sometimes possible to find 3/8" trim boards at the lumber mart and these are also satisfactory. It's also possible to remove material from a thicker board with the radial arm saw and the dado blades. Dado the thickness using cross cuts to about 13/32" and then sand the saw marks to make the 3/8" thickness board. See Figure 13-04 for an example.

MAKING DOORS & WINDOWS TO BE SECURED ON THE SIDES

Doors and windows to be secured on the sides should be cut to about 1/32" less than the vertical unit height so as not to touch the block above. They should be made about 1/4" wider than the nominal opening so that they'll penetrate about 1/8" into the Wall Bracket Block slots as shown in Figure 08-03. The doors can be exactly 1/8" thick since there won't be any slots to fall through.

MAKING WALL-BRACKET BLOCKS

If you don't have a router or prefer to secure the windows and doors from the sides, you can make slots a bit wider than those in FIGURE 08-01 with a saber saw. I found it difficult to control the saber saw when making samples for this book, so I made the jig shown in FIGURE 11-01. The only Wall-Bracket Block types needed are:

- WALL-BRACKET-SLOT1-1
  with a notch at one end for the end of a grid

- WALL-BRACKET-SLOT2-1
  with a notch at both ends for the middle of a grid

- WALL-BRACKET-SLOT2-2
  with a notch at both ends for the
  end of a grid when spanning grids

- WALL-BRACKET-SLOT1-3
  with a notch at one end for the end of a grid

- WALL-BRACKET-SLOT2-3
  with a notch at both ends for the middle of a grid

- WALL-BRACKET-SLOT1-5
  with a notch at one end for the end of a grid

Other configurations would rarely be needed since they'd be spanning a grid.

In FIGURE 11-01, the jig consists of a 1/4" plywood sheet with a slot for the blade and a hooked opening to accept the end of a clamp. I screwed two 3/4" boards to the plywood exactly 3/4" apart to make a track of sorts for a 23/32" wide block as shown. One board has the hooked opening for the clamp. On top of the 3/4" boards, I screwed two 1/4" plywood pieces about 5/32" to 3/16" further apart than the width of the saber saw frame so that I could control the notch width. Also on top of the 3/4" boards and behind the side guides, I screwed a stop for the saber saw frame so that it would penetrate 3/16" into the block to make a 3/16" deep, 5/32" wide slot. I made two crosswise marks so that I'd know where to place the front end of the block.

In FIGURE 11-02, a 1-1/2" block in the jig is being made into a WALL-BRACKET-SLOT2-1 Block like the one in the right foreground. The two small clamps on the left of the jig secure it to the table, and the larger clamp on the right holds the block against one side of the jig. If the block is much narrower than 3/4", shims like those in the left foreground are used to center the block in the jig. If it's wider, it violates the unit rule and must be sanded a bit. I didn't dado the notches for these examples. The notches would be dadoed before making the slots. The strange name is part of my elaborate naming convention.

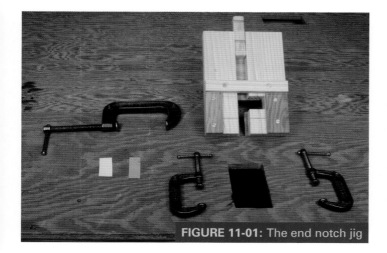

FIGURE 11-01: The end notch jig

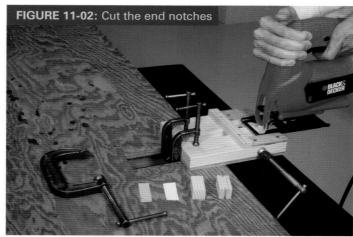

FIGURE 11-02: Cut the end notches

CHAPTER TWELVE
A LITTLE CITY

With the block types discussed so far, enough types are available to make a substantial building. Once you've determined the types you want to make, quantity becomes the issue. If you purchase a construction toy as a set from the store, your choices of type and quantity are pre-determined by the manufacturer. With the blocks, however, you must determine the types and quantities yourself based on the kinds of things you expect to build. Blocks as a hobby are therefore somewhat different from bricks or logs as a set.

Some block types are always in short supply while others have been in excess from the moment I made the first batch. I have untold extra BEAM-7-W Blocks, and these can normally be found in the bowels of larger displays as substitutes for BEAM-7-C Blocks. This issue led me to wonder about estimating block requirements, and I think there may be three ways to approach the problem.

The first is percentages. Of the block types introduced so far, those that account for more than one percent of the total are shown in the table below. Clay and sand colored blocks are included in the cement count. I originally had only wood colored blocks, but now that I include bases, the stone colors predominate. About two-thirds of all blocks are cement and one-third wood. The table shows that for each one hundred blocks, forty tend to be WALL-1 Blocks, of which twenty-three are cement and seventeen are wood. About five of the one hundred will be of types other than those in the table.

BLOCK TYPES	GREATER THAN 1% TOTAL	CEMENT	WOOD
BEAM-3	3	2	1
BEAM-3H	1	1	0
BEAM-5	1	1	0
BEAM-7	3	3	0
BEAM-7H	1	1	0
HEADER-3	1	0	1
WALK-1A	10	10	0
WALK-2A	4	4	0
WALK-3A	1	1	0
WALK-7A	2	2	0
WALL-1	40	23	17
WALL-1H	9	8	1
WALL-2	10	9	1
WALL-2H	3	3	0
WALL-3	4	0	4
WALL-7	1	0	1
WINDOW-3-HM	1	0	0
All other types	5	-	-
Total	100	-	-

FIGURE 12-01: A harbor island city

The second way to determine quantity is to tally the blocks in a construction and then estimate the number of constructions needed. The grid construction in FIGURE 06-09 is an example. Its counts include the supporting Wall and Beam Blocks as well as the Walk Blocks. If you're planning a scene with a base of four standard grids, you could quadruple the counts to arrive at an estimate. If the retirement cottage in FIGURE 09-01 were to be placed on top of a standard grid, the cottage and grid counts could be combined to reach a total. I always make a few extra blocks of each type to account for slight variations in the way I might build something.

The third way to estimate quantity is the simplest. I have only two Steeple Blocks and a limited number of Roadbed Blocks, so I can plan their placement exactly. Combining the three methods, and after a while intuition, a reasonable guess at quantity is possible. For me, the making of detailed architectural plans would violate the fun rule, but that's certainly a good way to ensure accuracy.

In FIGURE 12-01, Lowell is sitting in the middle of a little park. The scene appears to be a city built on top of an old island fort in the middle of a harbor. Antoine is opening a new restaurant on the third floor of the

73

FIGURE 12-02: A discussion on the plaza

FIGURE 12-03: The terraces

building at the left. He's waiting for Sternwood the accountant who seems more interested in Charlotte. Fulton is chasing a little coot into the docking basin. He runs a ferry between the island and the mainland.

The city sits on a pair of 2' x 4' tables and occupies nine grids. It's comprised entirely of the block types introduced so far. The cement base consumes at least as many blocks as the wooden buildings above it. Walk Blocks are used for the floors as evidenced by the cement colored bands at each level. The building in the rear has a small crossed dormer, and the building at the left has a clerestory roof. There are a number of roof terraces, all using Walk Blocks for the decks.

The WALK-7A-C Blocks in the front corner determine the "A" orientation. The WALK-7B-C Blocks forming the right fort wall are tied externally by WALL-2-C and WALK-2-C Blocks.

In FIGURE 12-02, Sternwood is touring the town. Bollards sufficiently small to secure the dory have yet to be introduced. The stairway consists of alternating courses of WALK-1A-C Blocks. The railing and walkway in the right foreground show how much space a railing consumes, a full three scale feet. Antoine is waiting impatiently on a terrace at the upper right. The rear building grids are tied at the window levels by WALL-

2-W Blocks. The overhang in the center rear above Sara shows the awkwardness of combining an overhang with an offset. The lawn is construction paper. At the lower left, clay colored blocks are used for decoration, and to the right of them is an ancient drain.

FIGURE 12-03 shows Antoine and Sternwood discussing the restaurant's location while customers wait impatiently on the rear terrace for it to open. Without already having gone through the restaurant, I don't know how they got there. The terrace overhang is WALK-7A-C Blocks. At their far end are WALK-2A-C Blocks to complete the seven unit grid. The weight of the building above keeps the works in place. Railings of both BEAM-7-C and BEAM-7H-C Blocks are shown. The stairway of alternating WALK-1A-C Blocks at the lower left by Oskar leads up to the plaza level. I try to have walkways entwined in the displays so that Oskar and his friends have a pleasant place to stroll.

FIGURE 12-04: The walkway overhang

FIGURE 12-05: The terraces and the walkway

FIGURE 12-04 shows Fulton ferrying Arthur back to the mainland. The coot shown is nameless. He or she later had so many identical water mates that I couldn't keep track. Antoine is through talking to Sternwood, but his potential customers have departed. The fort wall at the right is comprised of WALK-7B-C Blocks tied internally, and the wall at the left is WALK-7A-C Blocks tied externally. The overhang is comprised of Walk Blocks supported by BEAM-7-C Blocks. Shims are used to level the courses that are supported solely by notches. Three courses are required to secure an overhang in two orientations such as the one in the front corner. The first course of Beam Blocks supports the outer beam of the second course, and all the Beam Blocks of the second course support the outer beam of the third course. The Beam Blocks of the third course support the deck of WALK-7A-C Blocks on the fourth course. I used WINDOW-2-HM Blocks to indicate bathrooms and stairways or in places where a full window won't fit. In the center to the right of Rolfo is the other side of the awkward offset grids.

FIGURE 12-05 shows Antoine lamenting the failure of his endeavor. The restaurant on the level below has both inside and outside seating, and has attracted almost the entire village. Sternwood is leaving by the rear stairway, but seems to have missed the ferry. WALL-2-W ties are shown between the building grids. The tall building has a cloistered walkway on the plaza level.

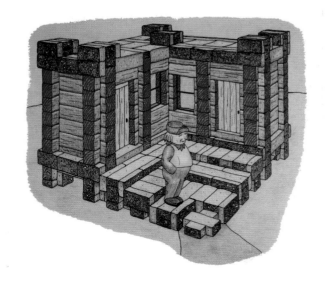

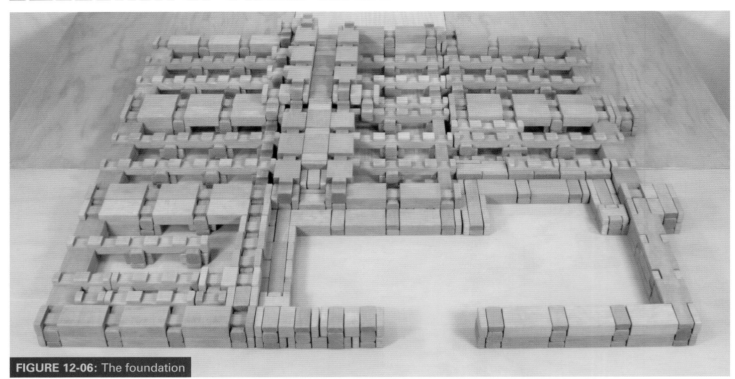

FIGURE 12-06: The foundation

FIGURE 12-06 shows the town plan and the first few courses. Except for the drain passageway from front to rear, only the framework of the lower grids is completed. The breakwater on the left side of the boat basin shows the use of WALK-2A-C and WALK-1A-C Blocks for walls that are not three, five, or seven units long. They're functioning more as bricks here, while the WALK-7A-C Blocks to the right are functioning more as logs.

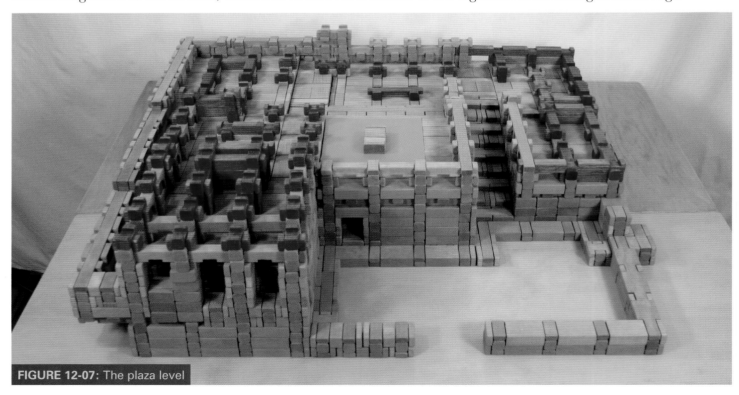

FIGURE 12-07: The plaza level

FIGURE 12-07 shows the completed grids of the plaza and first few courses of the buildings. Much of the first floor is open passageways. While the base grids are usually tied continuously at the corners, the building grids are usually tied only at the window levels or where doorways are adjacent to the grid ends.

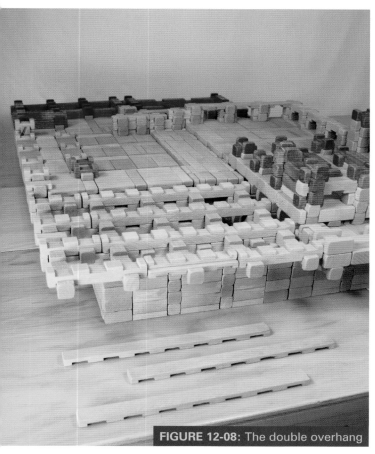

FIGURE 12-08: The double overhang

FIGURE 12-09: The plaza level headers

FIGURE 12-08 shows the crossed BEAM-7-C Blocks that support the corner overhang. The balanced back-to-back BEAM-3H-C Blocks in the foreground — slightly offset for clarity — are needed to complete the nine-unit span. The BEAM-7H-C Blocks in the water will fit between the Beam Blocks already in place, and they will steady the WALK-7A-C Blocks to be placed on top. FIGURE 12-04 shows an end view of the four courses in this corner.

FIGURE 12-09 shows some of the Header Blocks on the plaza level. Most of the Header Blocks at the lower right are in the middle of grids. This is needed because the doors and windows on the plaza level are set back from the building edges under porticos.

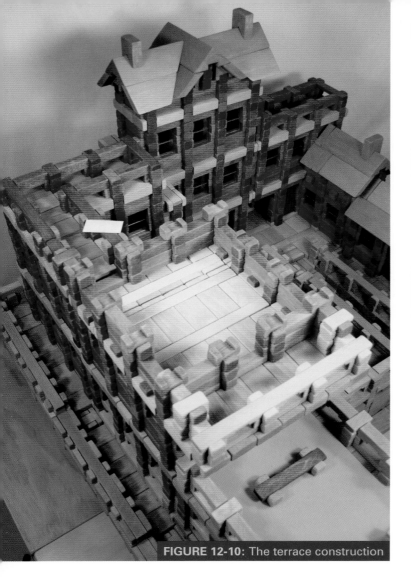

FIGURE 12-10: The terrace construction

FIGURE 12-11: The gable roofs

FIGURE 12-10 shows the floor and overhanging deck of Antoine's restaurant. The WALK-2A-C Blocks, mentioned in FIGURE 12-03, complete the nine-unit floor at the rear. Below and in front of the white shim, a BEAM-7-W Block is used to secure the tops of the WALK-2A-C Blocks and to support the seven-unit long wall and doorway above it. Ideally, a combined Beam-Footer Block would be used here to span the quarter-unit gap in the floor between the grids, but I have no such block; hence, the shim. A DOOR-5-W Block will sit on top of the BEAM-7-W Block. For me, erecting a complicated structure is two courses up and one down and then repeat until I get it right. Had I thought of the thicker Door Blocks and the thinner tab for the Footer Blocks when I first built this, the elaborate discussion above could have been avoided. The offset overhang below the rear terrace mentioned in FIGURE 12-02 took three hours to complete.

FIGURE 12-11 shows the use of shorter Roof Blocks as fillers. Both roofs have an overhang on only one end, so ROOF-SIDE-.5-T, ROOF-SIDE-1-T and ROOF-CAP-.5-T Blocks are used to add the half unit. Judicious Roof Block selection and placement reduces the possibility of having two blocks terminate in the same spot. I don't have any blocks to fill the quarter-unit gap where the ROOF-CAP Blocks meet the adjacent wall. Whether to make a block or accept a flaw is a constant issue with the blocks. The wall and plaza level deck in the foreground of FIGURE 12-02 illustrate another flaw. I was initially bothered by the need for a Beam Block just below the deck since it destroyed the smoothness of the wall. However, the solution seemed worse than the problem, so I've come to accept it. The solutions to these problems tend to violate the elemental rule. The harbor city scene is intended to show what can be done with only the basic block types. Sufficient quantities for such a creation would come over time.

SECTION TWO
A FEW MORE BLOCKS

CHAPTER THIRTEEN
HOME IMPROVEMENT BLOCKS

When I started writing this book, my thoughts were to document the blocks as I had made and used them. However, when I thought of a beginner staring at nothing but a 1" x 12" board, I realized that I had missed the mark. I didn't have any block types to build the house in FIGURE 09-01 without the foundation, the conglomeration in FIGURE 12-01 is a stretch for a child, and there's no way to get a vehicle from a table up to a display. As you may have gleaned from FIGURE 12-01, my goal for the blocks was to duplicate the brick construction in FIGURE 01-07, but I doubt that's what most folks would have in mind. Improvements are needed.

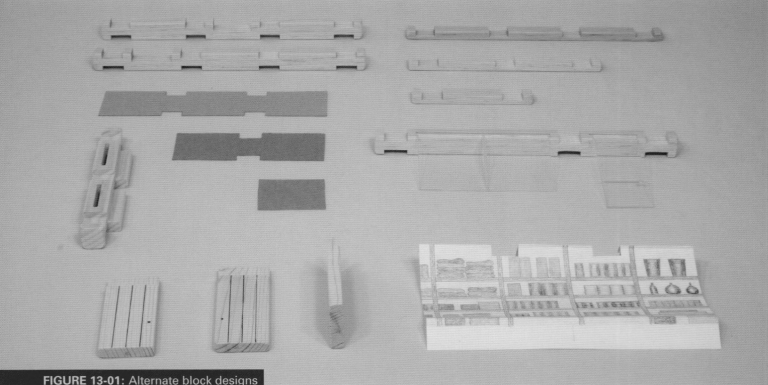

FIGURE 13-01: Alternate block designs

FIGURE 13-01 shows some home improvements that allow you to build structures without needing a grid underneath.

At the top right are WALL-7H, WALL-5H, and WALL-3H Blocks demanding to be stained in the cement color so they can be used for foundations on a table. I have none myself. Below the walls are WINDOW-3-3-VM and DOOR-4.5-CLR Blocks to be supported by the HEADER-SLOT1-SLOT3-7 Block, which

they're leaning against. This will allow a more modern storefront than I possess. I found that windows wider than one unit demand an interior, so I colored some paper to represent one, as shown at the lower right.

At the lower and middle left are examples of the thicker doors and the narrow tab Footer Block. Above the doors are some cardboard floors to make multi-story homes more complete. At the top left are WALL-FOOTER-END-7 and WALL-FOOTER-CTR-7

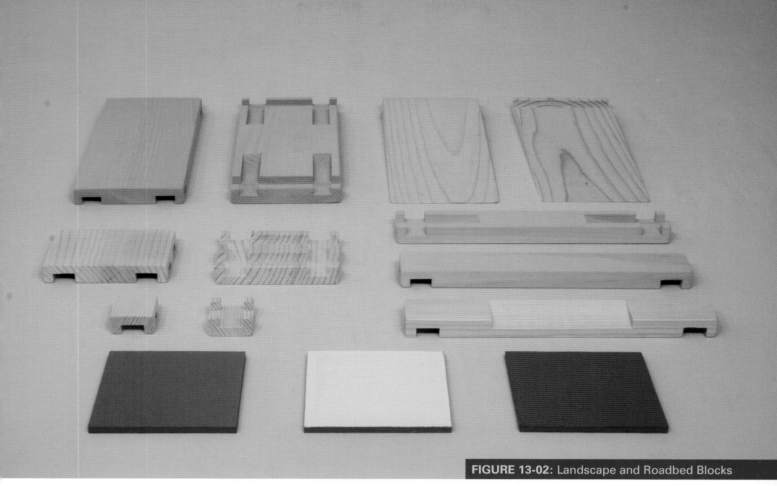

FIGURE 13-02: Landscape and Roadbed Blocks

Blocks that will keep an "A" orientation door off the lawn. You can choose either a wood or cement color for these, depending on your base preference. In case you're wondering, I imagine that a Wall Footer Block with three notches would be a WALL-FOOTER-END-CTR-END-7 Block. With a normal Header Block on top, the footer cutout requires doors a half vertical unit shorter than normal as shown at the bottom left. The DOOR-4.5 Block has a scale 6' 9" clearance, so as long as your figures are of reasonable proportions, they'll be happy.

Figure 13-02 shows some blocks that I already have and a few that I don't but thought are necessary.

At the top right are the top and bottom surfaces of RAMP-TAPERED-7-3-1 Blocks. These can lie flat on a grid for a one vertical unit drop, or they can hang on the cross support for a drop of two or three vertical units before behaving oddly. Below these are the top and bottom surfaces of ROADBED-7-1-SND Blocks, which I use to support the G Scale train. They're also suitable for streets and sidewalks, so I thought they'd be useful here. Below these is a ROADBED-DRIVEWAY-7-1 Block. If Roadbed Blocks are to function as both streets and walks, you'll need a way to get from one to the other in your automobile. This block drops the height one half of a vertical unit.

In the foreground are three LANDSCAPE-3-3-VAR Blocks. These are made from 7/32" Masonite sheets. Processed boards aren't made in thicknesses that are compatible with the blocks, so shims are needed if they're to be the same height as a vertical unit. My Landscape Blocks are stylized, as I found scale landscaping difficult with the blocks concept. Also, scale landscaping violates nearly all the rules I formulated. One surface and the edges are normally a grass color, and the other surface is either a dirt color or a water color. These are reversible blocks, and are painted rather than stained.

I mentioned in Chapter 6 that WALK-1A Blocks were good for making steps but were a bit wobbly. When I thought of what's needed for streets, I came up with the ROADBED-1-1 Block. To my amazement, these are stable when used as steps since they rest on crossed supports. Who knows what the pier in Figure 06-10 would have looked like had I known this when I built it. To the rear of these are ROADBED-2-3 Blocks that help fill in a grid. At the top left are the top and bottom surfaces of ROADBED-7-3-SND Blocks that are used to support the G scale train.

FIGURE 13-03
ROADBED & RAMP
BLOCK DIMENSIONS

ROADBED-1-1

BOTTOM VIEW

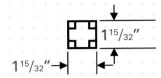

$1^{15}/_{32}''$

$1^{15}/_{32}''$

ROADBED-7-3

END VIEW   ## SIDE VIEW

$4^{15}/_{32}''$

$3/_8''$ $3/_4''$

GREATER THAN
$1^{1}/_2''$

ROADBED-7-3 TWO ABUTTING

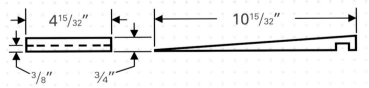

9" $1^{1}/_2''$ 9"

$10^{15}/_{32}''$ $10^{15}/_{32}''$

Roadbed Blocks can be of any reasonable dimensions, but bowing becomes an issue with lengths longer than one grid. Be sure the bow is convex. Ramp-Tapered Blocks can be wider or narrower than the example shown in 13-03.

The HEADER-SLOT1-SLOT3-7, WALL-FOOTER-CTR-7, WALL-FOOTER-END-7, WINDOW-3-3-VM, and DOOR-4.5-CLR Blocks are made in the same manner as other blocks of the corresponding type. The wide notch for the doors in the Wall-Footer Blocks is 3/8" deep and about 1-9/16" wide. The doorknob in the DOOR-4.5-CLR Block was made by lightly drilling a slight depression in the plastic using a drill press.

ROADBED-7-3-1

HIGH END VIEW   ## SIDE VIEW

$4^{15}/_{32}''$ $10^{15}/_{32}''$

$3/_8''$ $3/_4''$

NOTES:

The notch widths and the spacing between notches for Roadbed Blocks are the same as those for Wall Blocks, but the notch depths are exactly 3/8".

The lengthwise notches at the end of the Roadbed Blocks are made with the dado blades on the radial arm saw, and should extend at least 1-1/2" into the block at the 3/8" depth before tapering off due to the curve of the dado blades.

The RAMP-TAPERED Block has no lengthwise notches since they might emerge through the roadbed surface.

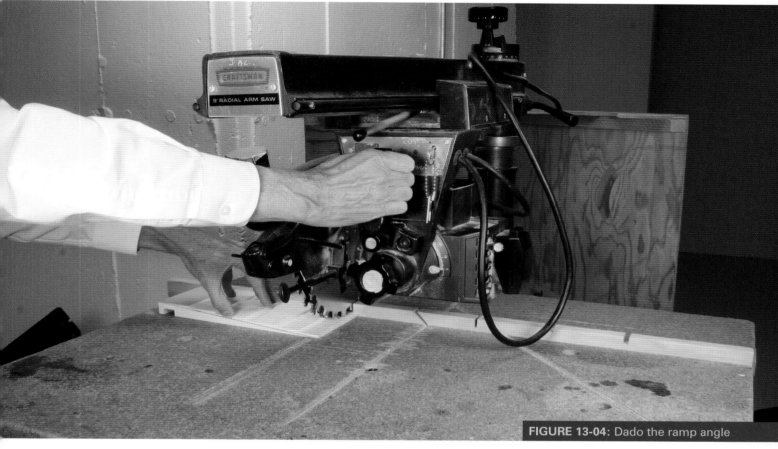

FIGURE 13-04: Dado the ramp angle

1. Rip a 3/4" thick board to 4-1/2" wide using the table saw.

2. Cut the board to 10-5/8" using the radial arm saw. The extra 1/8" beyond the grid length will allow for rounding the tapered end a bit to 10-1/2". I didn't allow for this in my sample, and the ramp is a tad shorter than I'd like.

3. Dado a 3/8" deep, 25/32" wide groove centered 3/4" from the end of the board using the radial arm saw. This is the same distance from the end as for a WALL-1 Block or one of any other length before the ends are sanded. I mark the board at 3/8" and 1-1/8", and then make sure that the outsides of dado blades fall outside of each mark.

4. Mark each lengthwise edge of the board from the top of the grooved end to the bottom of the non-grooved end; these marks determine the slope.

5. Dado most of the material above the marks using the radial arm saw. This reduces the amount to be removed by the belt sander. There's a tendency to be greedy here, but a RAMP-TAPERED-POTHOLE-7-3-1 Block is unpleasant for the little folks.

6. Sand the ramp down to the edge marks using the belt sander.

7. Touch the high end to the belt sander to reduce the length, and then round all the edges. Be careful not to round the taper beyond 10-1/2". The tapered end should cover any block or space below it, but not extend beyond the grid. You may want to use this block type as a sloped roof within a framework.

8. Stain the ramp in the same manner as other blocks. My Roadbed Blocks are a light tan color, and my Street Blocks are the same darker gray as my Roof Blocks.

MAKING ROADBED-1-1 & ROADBED-7-1 BLOCKS

ROADBED-1-1 Blocks absolutely must be made either along with a ROADBED-7-1 Block or in multiple side by side pairs for safety. The two types combined method is described here.

1. Rip the 3/4" board to 1-15/32" wide using the table saw.

2. Cut the board to 17" long using the radial arm saw. This length will make four ROADBED-1-1 Blocks and one ROADBED-7-1 Block with four 1/8" gaps for the final cutoff operation.

3. Dado the lengthwise grooves 3/8" deep and 25/32" wide using the radial arm saw as shown in FIGURE 10-14. This is done by pushing the block into the blades and then pulling it back. Note that the groove penetrates the ROADBED-7-1 Block only enough to accept a one unit block on its ends. Be sure not to push the board so far in that the anti-kickback arm is engaged. Only two or so ROADBED-1-1 Blocks should be appended on each end of the ROADBED-7-1 Block.

4. Dado the crosswise grooves using the radial arm saw; be sure to remember the 1/8" gaps for the final cutoff operation.

5. Cut off the ROADBED-1-1 Blocks using the radial arm saw.

6. Touch the ends of all the blocks to the belt sander to reduce their length and width, and then round the edges.

7. Stain the blocks in the same manner as other blocks.

MAKING ROADBED-2-3 BLOCKS

ROADBED-2-3 Blocks must be made either along with a ROADBED-7-3 Block or in multiples lengthwise for safety. The two types combined method is described here.

1. Rip the 3/4" board to 4-1/2" wide using the table saw. I've found that it's easier to measure with a nominal width board when making multiple dado cuts in one block.

2. Cut the board to 16-3/4" long using the radial arm saw. This length will make two ROADBED-2-3 Blocks and one ROADBED-7-3 Block with two 1/8" gaps for the final cutoff operation.

3. Dado the lengthwise grooves 3/8" deep and 25/32" wide using the radial arm saw as shown in FIGURE 10-14. This is done by pushing the block into the blades and then pulling it back. Only one ROADBED-2-3 Block should be appended on each end of the ROADBED-7-1 Block.

4. Dado the crosswise grooves using the radial arm saw; be sure to remember the 1/8" gaps for the final cutoff operation.

5. Cut off the ROADBED-2-3 Blocks using the radial arm saw.

6. Touch the ends and sides of all the blocks to the belt sander to reduce their length and width, and then round the edges.

7. Stain the blocks in the same manner as other blocks.

FIGURE 13-05: Dado the driveway angle

MAKING A ROADBED-7-1-DRIVEWAY BLOCK

This block is made from a completed ROADBED-7-1 Block. The middle three units — about 4-1/2" — are reduced to 3/8" on one edge. I made the jig shown at the top of FIGURE 02-02 to control the dado angle. The jig is a 3/8" thick board, which is as long as the width of the radial arm saw table. I sanded the board on the belt sander so that it tapers from 3/8" to nothing where the Driveway Block will be placed.

1. Clamp the jig to the radial arm saw table with the 3/8" edge toward the backstop, as shown in FIGURE 13-05.

2. Dado the taper using the radial arm saw. Allow a little extra material on the ramp so that the saw marks can be sanded.

3. Hand sand the surface to remove the saw marks. Note: The fun rule doesn't apply here.

MAKING LANDSCAPE BLOCKS

I was given a number of 7/32" Masonite sheets, so I used these for the Landscape Blocks. This thickness yields a heavy, stable block, so I expect to continue using it. The sheets were four feet square to start.

1. Cut the sheet to an exact width using a circular saw. This should be about 1/16" less than the nominal dimension so that adjacent sheets won't bind. Since Landscape Blocks are so large, it's important to make them as square as possible and to allow for error since you may fail. Be sure to consider the fun rule here. Also, Masonite is quite dusty, so I try to avoid major sanding operations.

2. Cut the sheet to an exact length or size using the radial arm saw. Landscape Blocks can be of any size and can also be freeform, but keep the unit and grid concepts in mind. For me, these are blocks and must behave as such. Odd sizes tend toward modules and violate the elemental rule. Some suggested sizes — measured in units — are listed below. Any of these can represent a lawn, a garden, or a pool. I name these LANDSCAPE-1-2-VAR, LANDSCAPE-1-3-VAR, etc. when making a Bill of Materials.

SIZE	COMMON USES
1 x 2	Tiny lawns around buildings or in the middle of a walkway
1 x 3	Tiny lawns around buildings or in the middle of a walkway
3 x 3	Small lawns
5 x 5	Small lawns either freestanding or surrounded by a full grid framework
5 x 7	Small lawns either freestanding or surrounded by a full grid framework
5 x 12	Large lawns either freestanding or surrounded by a two grid framework
7 x 7	Small freestanding lawns occupying a full grid
7 x 14	Large freestanding lawns occupying two full grids

CHAPTER FOURTEEN
A LITTLE TOWN

FIGURE 14-01: A little town

During the middle bricks period, I'd sometimes make a dozen or so small freestanding buildings and then slide them around my desk to make a compact downtown scene. The buildings were full-sized, but small. After I had arranged them tightly enough, I would push my little vehicles through the maze to create an urban traffic jam. In this scheme, the buildings represented various indeterminate stores, offices, and warehouses. Once I had sufficient bricks to make a city, I rarely again thought of making a town. FIGURE 12-01 clearly demonstrates that the same phenomenon recurred with the blocks. Once I discovered the grid, I stopped making the houses and concentrated on making the city.

When I re-thought this book in terms of a newcomer, I decided that the blocks ought to include more than just my preferences. The blocks introduced in Chapter 13 help fill the gap. FIGURE 14-01 shows an abandoned town that's been restored as a historic village. The site began as a fort, and the town grew up around it.

All the buildings except for the clay colored store in the center are resting on Landscape Blocks. The store interlocks with the grid construction beneath it. At the upper right, Sternwood is standing in front of a two-story house with a front parlor extension. Barely visible to its left is the old cement library, now a museum hosted by Sara. Antoine is inside the store, which now functions as the museum offices as well. Hannah acts as a tour guide for the entire village. Charlotte tells guests about the little cottage in the foreground that features an external chimney in the rear. To add a bit of excitement for children, Fulton offers rowboat rides.

The four structures on the left all lack doors and windows. Each of these can be made from a small collection of blocks that I call **"A Little Set"**. None of the blocks in this mini-collection are fragile, so the little set blocks would be suitable for a younger builder. In the middle foreground, Rolfo stands next to a two-story farmhouse with a shed extension for livestock. At the left is a primitive slope roofed coop manned by Oskar. Behind the coop, Arthur is in charge of the restored blockhouse. The blockhouse has an overhanging roof in one orientation. Barely visible in the center rear is the visitor center with a descending roof. Lowell greets the guests when there are any.

The village occupies an entire 5' x 5' table. The table holds five square grids with five units extra in each orientation. For the display, some grids are offset. The pond in the foreground is a LANDSCAPE-7-14-VAR Block occupying two full grids. Behind the pond is a RAMP-TAPERED-7-3-CLR Block to get vehicles to and from the display. Another ramp is located halfway along the street toward the rear. It's flanked by two ROADBED-7-1-SND Blocks. One end of each is raised half a vertical unit. A half-unit rise in a seven-unit block isn't a problem, but the ends don't mate as well as those of two Ramp Blocks. The road intersection is comprised of a ROADBED-7-3-SND Block and an assortment of ROADBED-2-3-CLR and ROADBED-1-1-CLR Blocks. Except for the foreground extension, the road is five units wide with a one-unit wide sidewalk on each side. In the center behind the store are LANDSCAPE-5-5-VAR Blocks acting as a pond and an unplanted garden. At the left rear and the right rear, Landscape Blocks are laid one atop another to make a slight rise. The green coloring on the block edges helps to make the transitions appear smoother.

FIGURE 14-02: The general store

FIGURE 14-02: This shows how brighter stone colors and larger windows help to modernize a building. The large window makes the interior visible such that an attraction like Antoine and the shelves becomes necessary. The upstairs interior is less demanding, but it does have a cardboard floor. The unstained blocks are the HEADER-SLOT1-SLOT3-7-CLR and WALL-FOOTER-END-7-CLR Blocks from Chapter 13. The farmhouse in the foreground shows the use of Roof-Side Blocks as shed dormers.

FIGURE 14-03: The town from the hill

FIGURE 14-03: This shows the village from the opposite direction. The museum in the center is comprised of smooth sided Walk Blocks. The visitor center on the right has a descending gable roof. When I made this, it occurred to me that a series of these roofs would look good on a hillside street. In the center foreground is the Driveway Block. Behind it, Rolfo is standing on a stairway of ROADBED-1-1-CLR Blocks which lead up to the blockhouse. The exterior wall of the display is tied externally on the left and internally on the right.

FIGURE 14-04: The Little Set buildings

FIGURE 14-04: Here are the Little Set buildings. Oskar's coop building is rather primitive, and its roof is simply WALL-5-W Blocks laid on a one vertical unit rise. With the loose notch spacing, a one unit rise isn't a problem for the longer blocks. The vacant notches are covered with loose WALL-1H-W Blocks. The stacked landscape panels on the left are LANDSCAPE-7-7-VAR, LANDSCAPE-7-5-VAR, and LANDSCAPE-7-3-VAR Blocks. The HEADER-7-C Block over the door and windows of the museum is a new color for headers and is usually used in basements. I used to use wood colored headers, but Oskar kept asking why they didn't rot. The exterior wall of the display consists of WALK-7B-C Blocks on the bottom and WALK-1A-C and WALK-2A-C Blocks above. In front of the coop, WALK-1A-C Blocks are used. Tying becomes dicey when only one vertical unit is available.

FIGURE 14-05: The main street

FIGURE 14-05: The rear of the store with the rear DOOR-5-GRN Block sitting on the cement base. The front door is a DOOR-4.5-CLR Block. It rests half a vertical unit off the base. If the store were standing on a Landscape Block, the five vertical unit door would look odd. The green stripe on the near edge of the plowed garden is the green edge of the Landscape Block. I can pretend that it's grass here, but the grass color would be less successful if the edge of the adjacent pond were exposed. Sternwood is standing on a flight of alternating WALK-1A-C Block steps.

FIGURE 14-06: The Little Set buildings dissected

FIGURES 14-06 & 14-07: Here are the buildings with the roofs and entourage removed. The flat roofs are WALK-7A-C Blocks supported by BEAM-3-C Blocks, and the gable roofs are supported in the same manner as the roof in FIGURE 07-03.

FIGURE 14-07: The roofs dissected

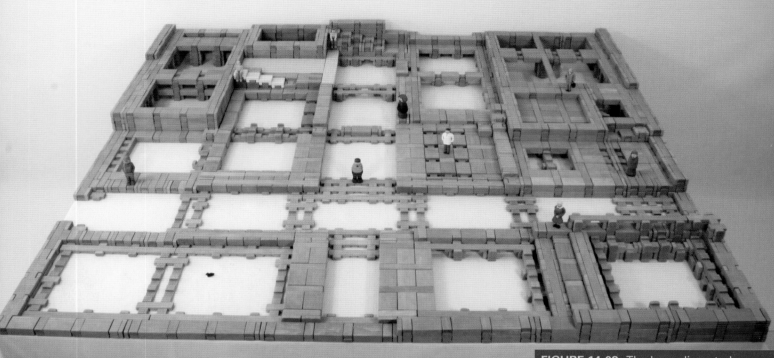

FIGURE 14-08: The base dissected

FIGURE 14-08: The grid framework. The grids in the left foreground enclosing the coot have only half a vertical unit available for tying. Each grid is held together at its corners, and adjacent grids are tied in the middle. The grid work in front of Rolfo holds the single and double Roadbed Blocks in place. Since Landscape Blocks are used instead of grid frameworks, only the outsides of most grids are completed. The grid under Antoine is complete since it supports the store. The grids in the vicinity of Sternwood are offset, which accounts for the odd constructions in that area. The grids in front of Sara are standard and are easier to assemble.

FIGURE 14-09

A LITTLE TOWN
BILL OF MATERIALS

FIGURE 14-09: The table is a Bill of Materials for the Little Set and the eight buildings in the display. If you have difficulty assembling the buildings from the photos, it may help to gather the blocks needed, assemble the structure, and then see what remains using the lawn mower engine repair method. Also, the buildings needn't be built exactly as shown.

BLOCK TYPE	A LITTLE SET	SHED AND YARD	HOUSE AND SHED	BLOCK HOUSE	VISITOR CENTER	COTTAGE	MODERN STORE	SMOOTH WALLED MUSEUM	TWO STORY HOUSE
BACKDROP							1		
BEAM-3-C							6	4	
BEAM-3-W	4		4	4	3	2			4
BEAM-3H-C							2	4	
BEAM-5-CLY							1		
BEAM-5-W	2			2					2
BEAM-5H-C								2	
CHIMNEY-1H-C	1		1		1				1
DOOR-4.5-CLR							1		
DOOR-5-GRN							1	2	
DOOR-5-W						1			1
FLOOR-CARDBOARD				1			1		1
FOOTER-SLOT1-SLOT3-7-CLR							1		
FOOTER-5-W									2
FOOTER-7-CLY							3		
HEADER-3-W						1			5
HEADER-5-W						2			3
HEADER-7-C								2	
ROOF-CAP-1.25-T									2
ROOF-CAP-2-T	1		1		1				1
ROOF-CAP-3-T						2			
ROOF-CAP-4-T	2		1		1				1
ROOF-SIDE-.5-T						2			2
ROOF-SIDE-2-T	4		2		2	3			4
ROOF-SIDE-4-T	6		4		2	1			2
WALK-1A-C						3		28	
WALK-1AH-C								4	
WALK-2A-C						9			
WALK-2AH-C								2	
WALK-3A-C								8	
WALK-3B-C								10	
WALK-7A-C							3	6	
WALL-FOOTER-END-7-CLR							1		
WALL-1-C						12	12	30	
WALL-1-CLY							71		
WALL-1-W	190	38	109	66	39	39			82
WALL-1H-C						3	6	10	
WALL-1H-CLY							4		
WALL-1H-W	18	17	14	18	2				1
WALL-2-C								2	
WALL-2-W									1
WALL-3-CLY							33		
WALL-3-W	17	7	15	16	13	11			17
WALL-3H-W	2	1	1	2	2				2
WALL-5-W	11	9	11	10	6	5			11
WALL-5H-W	2	1		1		2			1
WALL-7-CLY							4		
WALL-7-W	11			1					
WALL-7H-W	2	1	2	2					
WINDOW-2-HM						1	1		7
WINDOW-3-HM							3	5	3
WINDOW-3-3-VM							1		
TOTAL	**273**	**74**	**165**	**123**	**72**	**102**	**158**	**118**	**156**

Our voyage with the blocks is complete. However, I hope a few of you will remain and maybe add a cottage or wharf of your own. If you're twelve or older, I can't guarantee you'll find it within you to push an automobile through your creation, but perhaps you could imagine it.

BLOCK NAMING KEY

The block name uniquely describes a block type. The parts of the name are hyphenated and are structured according to the Block Name Structure Table below. Some parts use abbreviated codes, and these are described in the Code Description Table below. Examples of block names are at the bottom.

APPENDIX
NAME STRUCTURE TABLE

ENTRY	DESCRIPTION	EXAMPLE
SYSTEM	FOR BLOCK SYSTEMS	1
-		
SYSTEM VERSION		1
-		
NAME 1	BLOCK NAME	1
-		
BLOCK VERSION		2
-		
NAME 2	SECOND PART OF NAME	1
-		
NAME 3	THIRD PART OF NAME	1
-		
NAME 4	FORTH PART OF NAME	1
-		
NAME 5	FIFTH PART OF NAME	6
-		
LENGTH	IN UNITS	2
ORIENTATION	A, B, OR AB	3
HALF LENGTH		3
LEFT OR RIGHT	IF APPLICABLE	4
-		
WIDTH	IN UNITS	2
-		
HEIGHT	IN VERTICAL UNITS	2
-		
COLOR	FOR WOOD BLOCKS ONLY	1
MUNTINS	FOR WINDOWS ONLY	5

BLOCK NAMING EXAMPLES

EXAMPLE 1: ARC7-V2-RAILING-CLIP-BASE-FULL-SND

This block is part of the second version of a seven unit diameter Arc Block system. It's a full railing clip base and is sand colored. The "full" term implies the existence of a partial railing clip base block.

EXAMPLE 2: RAMP-V2-3-3-1-T

This is a basic block, and is the second version of a Ramp Block. It's three units long, three units wide, rises one vertical unit, and is tar colored.

EXAMPLE 3: WALK-1AH-C

This is a basic block which is one unit long. It's in the "A" orientation, is a half thickness block, and is cement colored.

EXAMPLE 4: ROADBED-ANGLE-1HL-SND

This block is part of a block system which has not yet had a second version. It's a half thickness angle shaped Roadbed Block and is one unit long. It's left facing when viewed from the tangent end with the notches facing up and is sand colored.

APPENDIX
CODE DESCRIPTION TABLE

CODE	DESCRIPTION
A	A ORIENTATION
AB	ORIENTATION CHANGE
B	B ORIENTATION
BOT	BOTTOM
C	CEMENT COLOR
CLSD	CLOSED
CLR	UNSTAINED
CLY	CLAY COLOR
CM	CROSSED MUNTINS
CTR	CENTER UNIT NOTCH
DBL	DOUBLE
DEC	DECORATIVE
END	END UNIT NOTCH
EXT	EXTENDED
H	HALF HEIGHT
HLF	HALF LENGTH
HM	HORIZONTAL MUNTIN
I	STRAIGHT
L	LEFT (FOR ANGLE)
L	L SHAPE (FOR TYPE)
LR	LEFT AND RIGHT
LRG	LARGE
NAR	NARROW
NM	NO MUNTINS
OPEN0	NO WINDOWS
OPEN1	ONE WINDOW
OPEN2	TWO WINDOWS
R	RIGHT
SGL	SINGLE
SLOT1	ONE SLOT (VERTICAL)
SLOT1	ONE UNIT SLOT (LENGTHWISE)
SLOT2	TWO SLOTS (VERTICAL)
SLOT3	THREE UNIT SLOT (LENGTHWISE)
SML	SMALL
SND	SAND COLOR
T	T SHAPE (FOR TYPE)
T	TAR COLOR (FOR COLOR)
VAR	VARIOUS
VM	VERTICAL MUNTIN
W	WOOD COLOR
WID	WIDE
X	CROSSED

EXAMPLE 5: WINDOW-3-HM

This is a basic block. It's three vertical units high and has a horizontal muntin.

EXAMPLE 6: WALL-FOOTER-END-CTR-END-7-C

This is a basic block that is used as a footer, and it has a one unit long notch in the second, forth, and sixth unit positions. It is seven units long.

EXAMPLE 7: FOOTER-SLOT1-SLOT3-7-CLY

This is a basic block. It has a one unit long slot in the second unit position and a three unit long slot in the forth through sixth unit positions when viewed with the tab in front and on the bottom. It is seven units long.

APPENDIX
BLOCK NAMES

CHAP = Chapter where the block is described
DIAG = Diagram exists for the block type
PHOTO = Photo exists for the block type

NAME	CHAP	DIAG	PHOTO
ADJUSTING-HOOK	8		8
BACKDROP-VAR	13		13
BEAM-3	5	5	5
BEAM-3H	5	5	5
BEAM-5	5		5
BEAM-5H	5		5
BEAM-7	5		5
BEAM-7H	5		5
CHIMNEY-1H	7		7
DOOR-4	9	9	9
DOOR-4.5	13		13
DOOR-5	9	9	9
FLOOR-VAR	13		13
FOOTER-3	8	8	8
FOOTER-5	8		8,13
FOOTER-7	8		8
HEADER-3	8		8
HEADER-5	8		8
HEADER-7	8		8
HEADER-SLOT1-SLOT3-7	13		13
LANDSCAPE-1-2	13		
LANDSCAPE-1-3	13		
LANDSCAPE-3-3	13		13
LANDSCAPE-5-5	13		14
LANDSCAPE-5-7	13		
LANDSCAPE-5-12	13		
LANDSCAPE-7-7	13		
LANDSCAPE-7-14	13		14
LANDSCAPE-VAR	13		
RAMP-TAPERED-7-3-1	13	13	13
ROADBED-1-1	13	13	13
ROADBED-2-3	13		13
ROADBED-7-1	13		13
ROADBED-7-3	13	13	13
ROADBED-DRIVEWAY-7-1	13		13
ROOF-CAP-.5	7		7
ROOF-CAP-.75	7		7
ROOF-CAP-1	7		7
ROOF-CAP-1.25	7		7
ROOF-CAP-2	7	7	7
ROOF-CAP-3	7		7
ROOF-CAP-4	7		7
ROOF-CAP-DORMER-1.75	7		7
ROOF-CAP-DORMER-2.75	7	7	7
ROOF-CAP-DORMER-3.75	7		7
ROOF-SIDE-.5	7		7
ROOF-SIDE-.75	7		7
ROOF-SIDE-1	7		7
ROOF-SIDE-1.25	7		7

NAME	CHAP	DIAG	PHOTO
ROOF-SIDE-2	7	7	7
ROOF-SIDE-3	7		7
ROOF-SIDE-4	7		7
ROOF-SIDE-DORMER-1.75L	7		7
ROOF-SIDE-DORMER-1.75R	7		7
ROOF-SIDE-DORMER-2.75L	7		7
ROOF-SIDE-DORMER-2.75R	7	7	7
SHIM-VAR	7		7
SILL-3	8	8	8
SILL-5	8		
SILL-7	8		
SPANNER-4	5	5	
SPANNER-5	5	5	
WALK-1A	6	6	6
WALK-1AH	6		6
WALK-2A	6		6
WALK-2AH	6		6
WALK-3A	6		6
WALK-3AH	6		
WALK-3B	6	6	6
WALK-3BH	6		6
WALK-5A	6		6
WALK-5BH	6		6
WALK-7A	6		6
WALK-7B	6		6
WALK-7BH	6		6
WALL-1	3,4	3,4	4
WALL-1H	4	4	4
WALL-2	4	4	4
WALL-2H	4		4
WALL-3	3,4	3,4	4
WALL-3H	4		4
WALL-5	4	4	4
WALL-5H	4		4
WALL-7	4	4	4
WALL-7H	4		4
WALL-BRACKET-SLOT1-1	11		
WALL-BRACKET-SLOT2-1	11		11
WALL-BRACKET-SLOT2-2	11		
WALL-BRACKET-SLOT1-3	11		
WALL-BRACKET-SLOT2-3	11		
WALL-BRACKET-SLOT1-5	11		
WALL-FOOTER-CTR-7	13		13
WALL-FOOTER-END-7	13		13
WALL-FOOTER-END-CTR-END-7	13		
WINDOW-2-HM	9	9	9
WINDOW-3-HM	9	9	9
WINDOW-3-3-VM	13		13